# My Book of
# Fossils

Author: Dr. Dean Lomax

**DK** | Penguin Random House

**Senior Editor** Roohi Sehgal
**Project Editors** Olivia Stanford, Radhika Haswani
**US Senior Editor** Shannon Beatty
**US Editor** Margaret Parrish
**Assistant Editor** Niharika Prabhakar
**Senior Art Editors** Ann Cannings, Nidhi Mehra
**Project Art Editor** Kanika Kalra
**Art Editor** Mohd Zishan
**Assistant Art Editor** Aishwariya Chattoraj
**Publishing Coordinator** Issy Walsh
**Jacket Designer** Rashika Kachroo
**DTP Designers** Sachin Gupta,
Syed Md Farhan, Vikram Singh
**Project Picture Researcher** Sakshi Saluja
**Production Editor** Dragana Puvacic
**Senior Production Controller** Isabell Schart
**Managing Editors** Jonathan Melmoth,
Monica Saigal
**Managing Art Editors** Diane Peyton Jones,
Romi Chakraborty
**Delhi Team Heads** Glenda Fernandes,
Malavika Talukder
**Deputy Art Director** Mabel Chan
**Publishing Director** Sarah Larter

First American Edition, 2022
Published in the United States by DK Publishing
1745 Broadway, 20th Floor, New York, NY 10019

# Contents

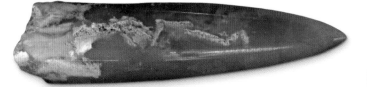

# What are fossils?

Fossils are the remains or evidence of ancient life that we can see today. Scientists who study fossils are called paleontologists. By examining fossils, we can discover the types of animals and plants that lived on Earth long ago.

Even the most delicate parts of an ancient animal can become fossilized, such as these tiny tail bones.

In the right conditions, fossils may preserve skin, fur, feathers, and even internal organs. The scales of this fish are still visible.

Usually, only small pieces of the original organism are found as fossils. However, some specimens can be completely preserved, such as this fossil fish, called Priscacara.

Some rare animal fossils are found with their last meal still inside their stomach.

# Great finds

Sometimes, amazing fossils are found that show us not just what an animal looked like, but also how it behaved. Certain fossils reveal how prehistoric animals cared for their young, how they built homes, what they ate for dinner, or even that they got sick.

This remarkable fossil captures a larger fish eating a smaller fish when they both died. The event has been frozen in time since the Paleogene Period.

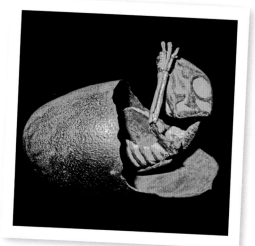

Eggs and babies of the dinosaur Maiasaura have been found inside a nesting ground. The babies were cared for by their parents.

# Types of fossil

Fossils come in all shapes and sizes—from tiny grains of pollen to gigantic dinosaur bones. There are two main types: body fossils, which preserve the hard parts of a life-form, and trace fossils, which are evidence of its existence.

## Trace fossils

Trace fossils record behaviors of ancient life. This can be in the form of tracks and trails, burrows and nests, and even fossilized poop, called coprolite.

Fossilized insect in amber

Fossil footprints are some of the most commonly found trace fossils.

Amber can preserve both body and trace fossils together.

Chirotherium footprint

Mammoth found in ice

This baby mammoth was discovered when ice in Russia melted.

## Not just rocks

Not all fossils are formed inside rocks. Sometimes organisms can become trapped in amber or frozen in ice. These methods of fossilization often preserve more delicate body parts, such as fur and skin.

# Body fossils

Body fossils are the direct remains of organisms that were once living, such as animals and plants. Usually, only hard parts, including bones, teeth, shells, and bark, fossilize.

Triceratops skull

This Triceratops skull is a perfect example of a body fossil. Both the bones and teeth are preserved.

Organisms may leave behind many trace fossils, but just one skeleton.

Megalodon tooth

Shark teeth are among the most common body fossils found in the world.

# Molds and casts

If an animal or plant becomes buried, its body parts might break down, leaving behind a space (mold) in the rock. This space may be filled with minerals to create a three-dimensional copy (cast) of the original life-form.

Mold fossil

Cast fossil

# Making a fossil

Not every life-form will become a fossil—in fact, it is very rare and conditions have to be just right. Even organisms that do become fossilized may take millions of years to be transformed.

## Ammonite

Ammonites were shelled sea creatures related to squid, and they are commonly found as fossils. Organisms must be quickly covered in sediment, such as mud and sand, for their remains to be preserved, which is more likely to happen underwater.

The soft parts of organisms rot away quickly and are not usually preserved.

Hard parts, such as shells, are most likely to fossilize before they break down.

Copal

Lignite

## Partly fossilized

Fossilization is a very long process. Plants or animals transform gradually and partly fossilized specimens can be found. For example, tree resin becomes copal before it hardens into amber, and before plants fossilize into solid coal they turn into lignite.

Fine details of the original shell may be lost over millions of years. - - - →

Any colors or patterns on the original specimen are usually lost during fossilization. - - →

## The oldest fossils are almost 3.5 billion years old!

## Rocks and minerals

To be preserved as a fossil, the parts of plants and animals must usually be replaced by minerals, which turn them into rock. Many fossils are made of the minerals calcite and quartz, as well as the rocks agate and phosphorite.

Agate

Calcite

Quartz

Phosphorite

# Fossil record

By studying how old fossils are, scientists can create a record of life on Earth. Fossils show us when and where ancient organisms lived. The long history of the planet is divided into eras, which are further split into shorter periods.

**Key**

- Early Earth
- Paleozoic Era
- Mesozoic Era
- Cenozoic Era

**MYA** Million years ago

Spriggina

**3,500–542 MYA**

### First life

For billions of years, only single-celled life existed. The first larger animals, such as Spriggina, looked unlike creatures today.

Pterodactylus

Herrerasaurus

Dimetrodon

| **201–146 MYA** | **252–201 MYA** | **299–252 MYA** |

### Jurassic

More types of small and large dinosaur evolved in the Jurassic. In the skies, pterosaurs, such as Pterodactylus, ruled.

### Triassic

The first dinosaurs, such as Herrerasaurus, appeared in the Triassic. So, too, did the first mammals, but they were small and shrewlike.

### Permian

Reptiles and mammal ancestors dominated in the Permian, including the huge Dimetrodon. However, most species became extinct at the end of the period.

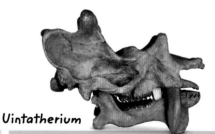

Uintatherium

Tyrannosaurus

| **146–66 MYA** | **66–23 MYA** |

### Cretaceous

A giant asteroid crashed into Earth at the end of the Cretaceous, killing the non-bird dinosaurs and many other species.

### Paleogene

Without non-bird dinosaurs to eat them, mammals, such as rhinoceros-like Uintatherium, got bigger. Birds also thrived and took over the air.

Elrathia

Conodonts

Baragwanathia

## 542–485 MYA

### Cambrian

An explosion of different types of life in the Cambrian Period brought many new animal groups, such as arthropods, including the trilobite Elrathia.

## 485–444 MYA

### Ordovician

Ocean life flourished in the Ordovician, including eel-like conodonts, which we know from their fossilized teeth. The first land plants also appeared.

## 444–419 MYA

### Silurian

In the Silurian, land plants, such as Baragwanathia, grew taller—although most were around knee height. Arthropods also moved onto the land.

Sphenopteris

Eusthenopteron

## 359–299 MYA

### Carboniferous

Ferns, such as Sphenopteris, grew across the planet during the Carboniferous. The Earth was lush with greenery and amphibians grew larger.

## 419–359 MYA

### Devonian

The first forests grew in the Devonian. More fish evolved, including Eusthenopteron, which had limblike fins and could breathe air.

Phorusrhacos

Mammuthus

## 23–3 MYA

### Neogene

Fossils show more familiar animals and plants in the Neogene Period. However, many creatures were supersized, such as the flightless, predatory bird Phorusrhacos.

## 3 MYA–today

### Quaternary

We live in the Quaternary Period. Recently extinct animals that existed early in the period, such as mammoths, can still be found as fossils.

## Digging through time

In many places, the deeper you dig, the older the rocks. Clear layers of different types of rock can tell us about big changes in the past, such as seas drying up or volcanoes exploding.

Rock layers

# Fossil sites

From deep inside deserts to the tops of the highest mountains, fossil sites are spread across the world—some in extreme environments. A few of these sites, such as the Burgess Shale, are famous for the extraordinary fossils they contain.

A team of paleontologists carefully excavates the fine shales in search of fossils. The fossils are so exceptional that even entire soft-bodied animals are preserved.

This spectacular fossil site is known as the Burgess Shale, and it is found in Canada. The first fossils were discovered here in 1909 by paleontologist Charles Doolittle Walcott.

Shale is a type of sedimentary rock. The shales at this site are from the Cambrian Period and contain fossils of some of the earliest animals ever to live.

Marrella was an early arthropod found by Walcott at this site in 1909.

## Famous fossil sites

Certain fossil sites have helped paleontologists understand how organisms have evolved over time. Such sites may reveal rare fossils, including those with preserved soft parts.

The Valley of the Moon, in Argentina, is most famous for containing fossils of the earliest-known dinosaurs. They are from the Triassic Period.

One of the most fossil-rich areas in the world, the Solnhofen Limestone in Germany, contains millions of Jurassic fossils, including some with preserved feathers.

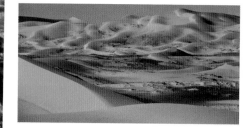

The Gobi Desert in China and Mongolia has revealed some spectacular finds from the Cretaceous, including the first dinosaur eggs and nests.

# Paleontology tools

Paleontologists use a variety of tools for finding and studying fossils. The equipment shown here is commonly used by fossil hunters. However, all fossil sites are different—sometimes only a keen eye is needed to spot something amazing!

Round brush

Flat brush

Brushes are used to clean dust from a fossil so that it's easier to identify what it is and understand how best to collect it.

Gloves

Goggles are one of the most important tools of all. They protect the eyes when hammering and chiseling rocks.

Goggles

A hard hat is good protection from falling rocks. Rocky hills and cliffs can be dangerous!

A strong backpack makes it easier to carry equipment, fossil finds, and food and water.

Hard hat

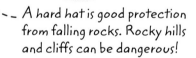

Cameras allow paleontologists to take pictures of fossils where they lie. This is vital at protected sites, where fossils cannot be collected.

Camera

Good fossil hunters take note of all their finds, including where and when they were discovered.

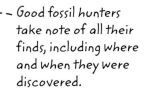
Pencil

Notebook

Clear plastic bags are essential for keeping fossils separated and safe.

Clear plastic bag

Trowels are used for lifting and moving loose items, such as sand.

Trowel

Backpack

Hammers can be used with chisels to break open rocks and carefully remove fossils from larger rocks.

Hammer

Chisel

## Fossil finds

Scientists read about the types of fossil they may find before visiting a site, so they know what to look for. Once a fossil is found, notes are made about it and it is studied closely.

An important step when finding a fossil is figuring out what species it is. Reading books, visiting museums, and asking experts can help with the identification.

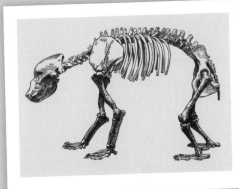

Sketching fossils is useful to capture details that may not be seen on photographs. Drawings can also help to better understand the structure of a fossil.

Microscopes are used to observe finer details of fossils that are usually too small to see. High-powered microscopes can reveal incredible features from the smallest fossils.

15

# Collecting fossils

Fossil hunting can be an exciting adventure. Just like traveling in a time machine, it allows you to step back through history and reveal a long-lost world. You may even discover a species new to science!

## Collecting safely

Make sure you have permission to visit any site and that you are allowed to collect fossils there. Follow these steps to stay safe:

- Always take an adult with you.
- Don't go near roads.
- Stay clear of any cliffs and never hammer at them.
- At beaches, be careful of slippery rocks and moving tides.
- Don't try to lift heavy rocks.
- Stay away from rivers, and watch out for slippery riverbanks.
- Wear safety goggles when hammering rocks.

## Where to find fossils?

Fossils are found around the world. They may be found on beaches, up hills, and even in backyards! Some fossil sites are protected by law. If you go fossil hunting, it is important to plan ahead and learn about the site you intend to visit.

Backyards

Hills

Beaches

# Caring for fossils

Success—you've found a fossil! Keep your fossils safe in containers, trays, or clear bags. Always include a label with key information, such as the date and location of discovery. If you are lucky to find many fossils, only take your favorites and leave the rest for others.

Wooden boxes like this can be useful for storing your fossil finds. - - - →

Mudstone is made up of fine clay or mud particles that commonly preserve fossils, such as this leaf.

Shale

Mudstone

Shale is the most common sedimentary rock, and it splits into thin sheets. It often contains fossils.

Limestone

mestone is mainly rmed from tiny pieces f ancient marine fossils, ch as corals and shells, essed hard together. - - -

# Rocks to look for

There are three types of rock: igneous, metamorphic, and sedimentary. Fossils are almost always found in sedimentary rocks, like those above, which formed from sediments, such as sand, being pressed together over millions of years.

# Stromatolite

## (stroh-MAT-oh-lite)

Stromatolites are among the oldest fossils on the planet. The earliest evidence of these rocky mounds dates back a staggering 3.5 billion years! They were formed by minute organisms called cyanobacteria, also known as blue-green algae.

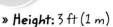
» **Height:** 3 ft (1 m)
» **Diet:** Photosynthesis
» **Period:** Precambrian to present
» **Location:** Worldwide

Each column shows how a colony of bacteria grew upward.

As groups of the tiny bacteria grew, layers of sand and mud became stuck to them. This sediment eventually transformed into rock.

Stromatolites in Shark Bay, Australia

## Living rocks

Stromatolites were once found throughout the world, but are rare today. In 1956, a site called Hamelin Pool in Shark Bay in western Australia was discovered; here, a giant colony of living stromatolites was found.

Some stromatolites have a mushroomlike shape.

# Cooksonia

## (COOK-so-NEE-ah)

Cooksonia was one of the earliest land plants, but, surprisingly, it did not have any roots, leaves, or flowers. The first Cooksonia fossils were found inside a quarry in Wales and were named in 1937.

**Fact file**

» **Height:** 4 in (10 cm)
» **Reproduction:** Spores
» **Period:** Silurian to Devonian
» **Location:** Worldwide

At the top of each branch was an oval-shaped bag called a sporangium, which contained spores.

A sturdy stem supported the plant and allowed it to grow upright.

Cooksonia fossils can be identified by their Y-shaped branches. Some Cooksonia had multiple branches.

Cooksonia was a very simple-looking plant. It had a single stem and few branches.

## Seedlike spores

Spores are the reproductive cells in certain types of fungi, lichens, and plants—including ferns and mosses. They are extremely small, but just like seeds, each one is capable of growing into a new plant.

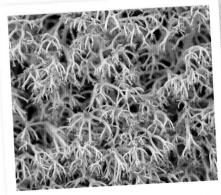

Reindeer lichen with pink sporangia

# Zamites

## (za-MY-teez)

Zamites is known mostly from large fossil leaves. The shape of the leaves closely resembles the modern cycad, Zamia, which the name Zamites comes from, but this plant actually belonged to an extinct group called bennettitales.

Fact file

» **Leaf length:** 20 in (50 cm)
» **Reproduction:** Flowerlike cones
» **Period:** Triassic to Cretaceous
» **Location:** Worldwide

Each leaf had a long, strong stem that attached it to the plant's trunk.

The leaves were divided into finely pointed leaflets that varied in length.

Zamites leaves have been found in the same rocks as dinosaur bones and footprints. They were likely to have been eaten by herbivorous dinosaurs.

Cycad cones

## Flowers or cones?

Cycads produce pollen and seeds in cones. Some bennettitales produced seeds in cones, too, but their cones were more flowerlike.

When alive, most of Zamites' leaves were clustered together at the top of its trunk.

# Pecopteris
## (peh-KOP-ter-is)

Leafy ferns grew everywhere in the Carboniferous Period. Pecopteris was a tree fern that resembled a palm tree, having a tall, straight trunk with a spray of many fronds at the top.

Hundreds of species of Pecopteris have been identified. Features, such as the shape of the fossil leaves, are used to identify a specific type.

Each leaf was divided into leaflets, which in some Pecopteris species looked similar to the teeth on a comb. Pecopteris means "comb fern."

Tiny seedlike spores would have been present on the underside of each leaflet.

A favorite of prehistoric herbivores, the oldest fossil ferns date back to the Devonian Period.

## Plant detective

Different parts of fossil plants are often given separate names, as it is hard to tell which belong together. For example, Psaronius (sa-ROH-nee-uss) is the name given to certain tree trunks, but some Pecopteris fronds may have grown on them.

*Psaronius trunk fossil*

21

# Lepidodendron

## (leppy-doe-DEN-dron)

Lepidodendron, a giant among prehistoric plants, is related to smaller, living club mosses. It formed vast, tropical forests around swamps and rivers and gave shelter to many early animals, such as small reptiles and insects.

Fact file
» **Height:** 165 ft (50 m)
» **Reproduction:** Cones with spores
» **Period:** Carboniferous to Permian
» **Location:** Worldwide

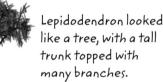

Lepidodendron looked like a tree, with a tall trunk topped with many branches.

Lepidodendron means "scale tree." It is named after the pattern on its bark, which looks like the scales on a snake.

As Lepidodendron grew, its leaves fell off, leaving a diamond-shaped pattern of scars where they had attached to the plant.

## Rocks from plants

Coal is a rock made from the remains of ancient plants. Most of the world's coal comes from Carboniferous forests. When plants, including Lepidodendron, died and became buried in swamps, they fossilized into coal.

The tall trunk was anchored into the ground by thick, rootlike structures called Stigmaria.

**Coal**

22

# Porana

## (por-AH-na)

Porana is a type of flower known from both fossil and living species. Flowering plants appeared at least 130 million years ago and are the most successful land plants today. This fossil flower is around 10 million years old.

### Fact file

» **Flower length:** 2 in (4 cm)
» **Reproduction:** Seeds
» **Period:** Neogene to present
» **Location:** Asia, Europe, and North America

In life, five large petals were brightly colored to attract insects for pollination.

## A world without flowers

Today, flowering plants are found worldwide, however, the first flowers only evolved in the Cretaceous Period. This means flowers appeared long after many familiar dinosaurs, such as Stegosaurus.

Fossil flowers may also show fine structures, such as veins, which help scientists to identify the species.

Insect pollination helped the first flowers to spread across the world.

There were no flowers in the Jurassic Period.

# Woodocrinus

## (wood-oh-KRY-nuss)

With a long stem and flowerlike head, Woodocrinus may have looked like a plant, but it was actually a type of sea animal called a crinoid. Crinoids are related to sea stars and sea urchins. Fossils show they appeared about 485 million years ago.

» **Length:** 20 in (50 cm)
» **Diet:** Carnivore
» **Period:** Carboniferous
» **Location:** Europe

The cup-shaped head was made of 20 feathery arms and is called a calyx. The arms filtered tiny prey from the water.

Crinoid stems are made up of many pieces, known as ossicles, which are common fossils.

Most Woodocrinus fossils have been found in Scotland.

## Sailing crinoids

One species of crinoid, Seirocrinus (sai-roh-KRY-nuss), from the Jurassic Period, attached itself to floating driftwood. The wood acted like a barge, with the crinoids as passengers. The largest fossil Seirocrinus barge found is longer than a school bus!

Seirocrinus barge

# Rhizopoterion

**(RY-zo-po-TEH-ree-on)**

Rhizopoterion was a type of sponge that lived on the seabed in the deep ocean. It belonged to a large group of sponges that are still alive today—they are also known as "glass sponges."

Fact file

» **Length:** 4 in (10 cm)
» **Diet:** Carnivore
» **Period:** Cretaceous
» **Location:** Europe

Just like modern glass sponges, the meshlike skeleton of Rhizopoterion was made from the same material as glass.

Rhizopoterion usually had a cone or funnel-like shape that narrowed toward the base. It stood upright on the seabed.

Tiny holes, called ostia, were used to take in water, which was then pushed out of the top of the sponge.

Living sponges can absorb and hold a lot of water, just like a bath sponge.

## Modern sponge

Sponges are filter feeders that eat microscopic organisms, such as plankton. They were some of the earliest animals to evolve, and more than 8,000 species can be found today.

A living sponge

# Thecosmilia

## (thee-koh-SMILE-ee-a)

Thecosmilia was a species of coral that lived on ancient reefs in warm, shallow water. It grew in large colonies, with each coral animal, called a polyp, making its home in a cuplike structure.

» **Height:** 6 in (15 cm)
» **Diet:** Carnivore
» **Period:** Triassic to Cretaceous
» **Location:** Worldwide

The radiating lines within each cup are called septa. The polyp was attached to these.

Each cup is called a corallite. This is where a single, soft-bodied coral animal, or polyp, lived.

The corallites of Thecosmilia were spaced apart. They made up the coral's hard skeleton.

## Packed together

Septastrea (sep-ta-STREE-a) is another fossil coral that belonged to the same group as Thecosmilia, nicknamed "stony corals." However, the corallites in Septastrea were much closer to each other.

Septastrea fossil

Calcite        Aragonite

The skeleton of a coral is made of the minerals calcite or aragonite.

# Pygurus
## (PY-gur-uss)

Pygurus was a type of sea creature called a sea urchin. It belonged to a group of invertebrates known as echinoderms, which also includes sea stars. The oldest sea-urchin fossils are more than 400 million years old.

» **Length:** 5 in (12 cm)
» **Diet:** Omnivore
» **Period:** Jurassic to Cretaceous
» **Location:** Worldwide

Many sea urchins have sharp spines for defense, like spiked porcupines.

A star shape is found on all sea-urchin skeletons. It shows where the urchin's breathing organs were.

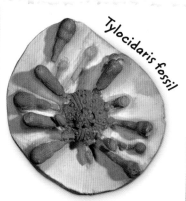

Tylocidaris fossil

## Thick spines

Tylocidaris (TIE-low-sih-DAR-iss) was an unusual sea urchin. It had a small body with thick, club-shaped spines, rather than a large body with lots of tiny, needlelike spines.

The round, hard skeleton of a sea urchin is called a test. In life, hundreds of tiny tube feet stuck out of it and were used to crawl... very slowly!

Modern sea urchins are found across the world, living on the ocean floor. When they die, their spines usually fall off.

# Didymograptus

**(did-ee-moh-GRAP-tuss)**

This strange-looking fossil may appear like scratchings on a rock, but Didymograptus was a graptolite—a type of invertebrate made up of colonies of tiny animals called zooids. It lived in the sea and fed on plankton.

Graptolite means "written rock," as many fossils resemble carvings.

Didymograptus had two long branches. Both had a row of toothlike structures, in which the zooids lived.

## Floating free

Graptolites appeared a little over 500 million years ago and were widespread in prehistoric oceans. Some species lived on the seabed, but others, such as Diplograptus (dip-low-GRAP-tuss), floated around in the water.

The odd body of the graptolite is called a tubarium and can be thought of as a house that the zooids built to protect themselves.

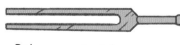

Didymograptus is known as a "tuning fork" graptolite because its fossils are shaped like a tool called a tuning fork.

Diplograptus

# Tibia

## (TIB-ee-a)

Even though it is millions of years old, this Tibia sea snail fossil looks like it was alive recently. In fact, Tibia still exist today. Snails are gastropods—a group of invertebrates that appeared more than 500 million years ago.

The long, narrow spike at the front end of the shell was hollow. It contained a sensory organ used to find food.

A pointed, twisting shell, called a spire, protected the snail from predators.

A large opening was where the squishy snail extended its "foot" to crawl around.

Many Tibia fossils have been found inside a quarry alongside basalt, a type of volcanic rock.

## Colorful shells

Gastropod shells come in a wide variety of colors, often with distinct patterns. However, markings and colors are almost always lost during fossilization.

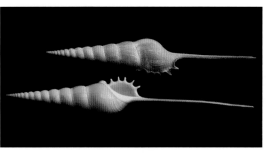

Living Tibia

# Hallucigenia

## (ha-lucy-JEAN-ee-a)

Hallucigenia has puzzled paleontologists since it was found at the Burgess Shale fossil site in Canada over 100 years ago. This wormlike animal had spikes on its back that were first thought to be its legs!

## Bizarre animal

It is still not certain what type of animal Hallucigenia was, because its soft body is often not well-preserved. However, it may be related to modern velvet worms.

Hallucigenia

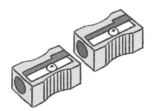

Hallucigenia could grow to just longer than two pencil sharpeners.

—Thin legs with claws were used to walk, but the front legs had no claws.

—Seven pairs of long, sharp spikes on Hallucigenia's back may have been for defense.

# Tullimonstrum

**(tull-ee-MON-strum)**

First discovered in the 1950s, Tullimonstrum is also known as the "Tully monster." Scientists disagree on what kind of animal this strange-looking creature was. Some even think it may have been a bizarre type of fish.

» **Length:** 14 in (35 cm)
» **Diet:** Carnivore
» **Period:** Carboniferous
» **Location:** North America

Tullimonstrum's eyes were found at the ends of a long bar on its head.

Thin, vertical fins on the body and tail were rippled to help Tullimonstrum swim.

Long mouthparts had a claw at the end filled with teeth. This was used to grab prey.

## Odd invertebrates

Some early invertebrates looked so strange that they could easily be thought of as aliens. Like Tullimonstrum, Opabinia (oh-pa-BIN-ee-a) had long mouthparts ending in a claw, but it also had five eyes on stalks!

Tullimonstrum was an unusual animal. This reconstruction shows how it might have looked in life.

Opabinia

# Trilobites

## (TRY-low-bites)

Trilobites were a group of marine arthropods—the group that contains insects and crustaceans—that appeared more than half a billion years ago. All trilobites were divided into three main parts, including the cephalon (head), thorax (body), and pygidium (tail).

> **More than 20,000 different types of trilobite are known.**

**Fact file**

- » **Length:** 28 in (70 cm)
- » **Diet:** Carnivore
- » **Period:** Ordovician
- » **Location:** North America

## Isotelus
### (eye-so-TELL-us)

Paleontologists have identified multiple species of Isotelus, including the largest species of trilobite known so far, Isotelus rex. This species was as long as a house cat!

This fossil is Isotelus maximus. It is the state fossil of Ohio.

Spines sticking out of this trilobite's back were used for defense.

**Fact file**

- » **Length:** 2½ in (6 cm)
- » **Diet:** Carnivore
- » **Period:** Devonian
- » **Location:** Africa

## Erbenochile
### (er-BEN-oh-CHILL-ee)

The first thing you might notice about Erbenochile are its large, towerlike eyes. They pointed upward and gave this trilobite better all-around vision.

# Asaphus
## (A-sa-fuss)

Many types of trilobite, such as Asaphus, were able to roll their entire bodies into balls. This helped to protect them from being attacked.

*Eyes on the ends of long stalks helped this species to detect predators and prey.*

*Some paleontologists think the prongs may have been used for fighting other trilobites.*

# Walliserops
## (WALL-ee-SERR-ops)

This trilobite was unusual because it had a forklike structure on its head. The prongs were possibly used for display, to attract mates, or to help the animal feel its way around.

*This trilobite's delicate legs and antennae are still visible.*

# Triarthrus
## (try-ARTH-russ)

Triarthrus trilobites are among the best preserved in the world. At a special site in New York State, many intricate specimens have been found—some even with eggs!

# Pterygotus

## (terry-GOAT-us)

Eurypterids, also called "sea scorpions," sound scary, but these creatures died out more than 250 million years ago. Pterygotus was first found in the 1830s, and thousands of its fossils have been discovered since then.

Fact file

» **Length:** 6 ft (1.7 m)
» **Diet:** Carnivore
» **Period:** Silurian to Devonian
» **Location:** Europe and North America

A fan-shaped tail, called a telson, probably worked like a rudder, to help steer when swimming.

Two long appendages with spiked pincers at the end were used to grab and tear up prey.

The body was segmented to allow it to bend. As Pterygotus grew larger, it shed its hard skin in a process called molting.

A pair of paddlelike legs were used for swimming.

Originally, it was thought that Pterygotus was a large fish, and its name means "winged fish."

## Underwater predator

Supersized sea scorpions, such as Pterygotus, were among the top predators in prehistoric seas. They dined on fish and arthropods, including trilobites.

Pterygotus

# Archimedes

## (ark-i-MEE-deez)

This fossil doesn't look like it belongs to an animal, but Archimedes was a type of invertebrate, called a bryozoan. The spiral structure was created by a colony of microscopic creatures to live in, like a coral.

### Fact file

» **Height:** 3 ft (1 m)
» **Diet:** Omnivore
» **Period:** Carboniferous to Permian
» **Location:** Worldwide

The screwlike skeleton supported a colony of animals, called zooids. It stood upright on the seafloor.

Bryozoan feeding fronds are commonly found as fossils.

The oldest bryozoan fossil is around 485 million years old.

## Bryozoans

Many types of bryozoan resemble corals and plants, and they are also known as "moss animals." Found around the world today, there are more than 5,000 living species.

Archimedes was a filter-feeder that strained food particles from seawater. To do this, it extended frondlike feeding arms from the main skeleton.

Archimedes was named after the Archimedes screw, a type of water pump.

Living bryozoan

35

# Aviculopecten

## (a-VIK-you-low-PECK-ten)

Aviculopecten looked like a seashell that you would find on a beach. It belonged to the same large group of animals as oysters and clams, called bivalves, which live underwater inside a hard shell made of two halves.

**Fact file**

» **Length:** $2^1/_2$ in (6 cm)
» **Diet:** Omnivore
» **Period:** Devonian to Permian
» **Location:** Worldwide

A hinge at the pointed end of the shell allowed Aviculopecten to open and extend its tentacles to trap tiny organisms.

This fan-shaped bivalve had several strong ribs that extended to the sides of the shell.

**Bivalves appeared more than 500 million years ago.**

## Fossilized pearls

Some bivalve fossils have been found with pearls inside. The oldest fossil pearls are more than 200 million years old—and can still look like shiny gemstones! One of the largest fossil pearls known measured 2 in (5 cm) wide.

Fossil pearls

The zigzag stripes on Aviculopecten's shell may have helped it to blend into its environment and hide from predators.

Bivalves and gastropods, such as snails, are both types of mollusk.

# Meganeura

## (MEGA-new-ra)

Although this fossil looks like it is of a dragonfly, Meganeura was, in fact, a closely related insect called a griffin fly. These bird-sized predators were the largest insects to have ever lived.

### Fact file

» **Wingspan:** 28 in (70 cm)
» **Diet:** Carnivore
» **Period:** Carboniferous
» **Location:** Europe

Meganeura's large eyes detected fast-moving prey, which it caught with its long, spiny legs.

Each wing was attached to the body by a hinge. The four wings could move independently, which helped Meganeura change direction quickly.

Most Meganeura fossils show the beautifully detailed veins that strengthened the wings.

The long, slender body was probably brightly colored when the insect was alive.

## Ruler of the skies

Insects were the first animals to evolve to fly. This was long before birds, bats, or even the flying reptiles, pterosaurs.
For millions of years, griffin flies dominated the skies as the top predators.

Meganeura

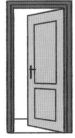

Giant Meganeura would only just be able to fly through most doorways.

# Cyrtospirifer

## (ser-toh-SPIH-rih-fer)

Cyrtospirifer was a brachiopod. These soft-bodied animals have a hard shell and live in the sea. Brachiopods were the most common shelled invertebrates during the Paleozoic Era, with thousands of fossil species identified. They still exist today!

» **Width:** 2¹/₂ in (6 cm)
» **Diet:** Omnivore
» **Period:** Devonian
» **Location:** Worldwide

Some species of brachiopod resemble oil lamps and are also called "lamp shells."

Brachiopods have an outer shell made of two halves, called valves.

Cyrtospirifer had deep grooves in its shell. These can help to identify which species it belonged to.

The two valves were joined at a hinge, which allowed the shell to open.

Brachiopods look very similar to bivalves, such as this clam, but they are different kinds of animal.

## Filter feeder

Brachiopods filter microscopic food, such as plankton, from the water. They have a special structure called a brachidium that supports their coiled feeding arms.

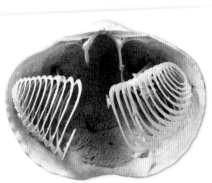

**Fossil brachidium in shell**

# Cylindroteuthis

## (si-lin-droh-TOO-thiss)

Cylindroteuthis was a squidlike creature called a belemnite. Belemnite fossils are common in marine rocks from the Mesozoic Era. Rare examples have been found with their arms still wrapped around fossil fish, which they ate.

Belemnite fossils have been found inside the stomach of a Jurassic shark!

Belemnites had a cone-shaped structure called a phragmocone in their bodies. This helped the animal to float.

A long, pointed end is the remains of the animal's hard internal skeleton, called a guard. It is made of the mineral calcite.

## Ink defense

Just like squid and octopuses today, belemnites could squirt ink at predators if they felt threatened. Some belemnite fossils have even been found with preserved ink sacs.

Belemnite guard fossils are very common, and they are regularly mistaken for dinosaur teeth.

Belemnite squirting ink

# Ammonites

## (AM-oh-nites)

Ammonites are an extinct group of marine animals related to octopuses and squid. They lived their entire lives inside shells, similar to snails. Their fossilized shells are found worldwide and range from ½ in (1 cm) across to more than 6½ ft (2 m)!

Ammonites went extinct at a similar time to the non-bird dinosaurs.

**Fact file**

» **Length:** 3 in (7 cm)
» **Diet:** Carnivore
» **Period:** Jurassic
» **Location:** Worldwide

Most ammonites, such as Dactylioceras, had coiled shells. Their arms and tentacles poked out of the wide end of the shell.

## Dactylioceras
### (DACK-till-ee-oh-SAIR-us)

Dactylioceras fossils were once known as "snakestones" because they looked like coiled snakes turned to stone. Some people even carved snake heads onto them.

The twists and turns of this ammonite make it one of the strangest species known.

**Fact file**

» **Length:** 5 in (12 cm)
» **Diet:** Carnivore
» **Period:** Cretaceous
» **Location:** Asia and North America

## Nipponites
### (NIP-oh-nites)

Nipponites is a type of ammonite called a heteromorph. Rather than having a spiral-shaped shell, these ammonites had shells that were straight, twisted, or oddly coiled.

» **Length:** 20 in (50 cm)
» **Diet:** Carnivore
» **Period:** Cretaceous
» **Location:** Africa and Europe

# Ancyloceras
## (an-see-low-SAIR-us)

This hook-shaped ammonite probably swam with its coiled end at the top, while its eyes and arms poked out of the shell entrance.

*The ammonite's body was covered in thin, closely spaced ridges.*

*In some species only the male or female had spines, which may have been used for display.*

**Fact file**

» **Length:** 24 in (60 cm)
» **Diet:** Carnivore
» **Period:** Cretaceous
» **Location:** Worldwide

# Crioceratites
## (kree-oh-sair-a-TITES)

Paleontologists have identified many species of Crioceratites. Some of them, like this one, were covered in large spines that served as protection against predators.

**Fact file**

» **Length:** 6 in (15 cm)
» **Diet:** Carnivore
» **Period:** Jurassic
» **Location:** Europe

# Kosmoceras
## (koz-moh-SAIR-us)

Many fossils of Kosmoceras preserve the original shell, like this one. The long, pointed part of the shell is known as a lappet and is only found in males.

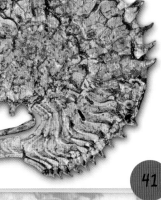

*We know this fossil belonged to a male Kosmoceras because it has a lappet.*

41

# Gemstone fossils

You might think all fossils look like rocks, but under certain conditions, organisms can be totally transformed into beautiful, often brightly colored, fossils. Some of these types of fossils preserve the original life-form in amazing detail.

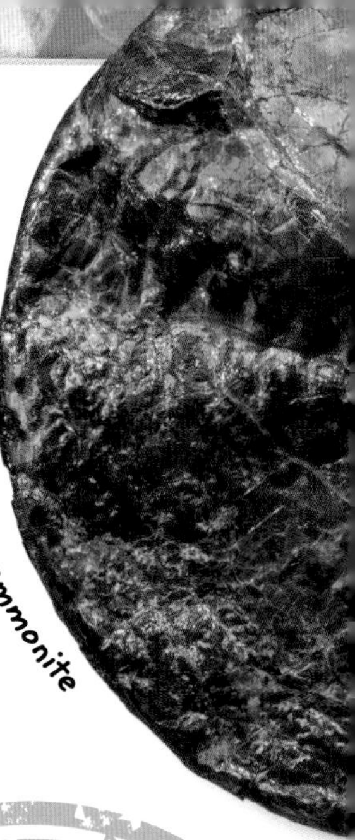

Ammolite ammonite

Pyrite belemnite

An opalized plesiosaur skeleton was found in 1987 and nicknamed "Eric."

This piece of a belemnite's internal shell, called a phragmocone, is preserved in the shiny mineral pyrite, also known as fool's gold.

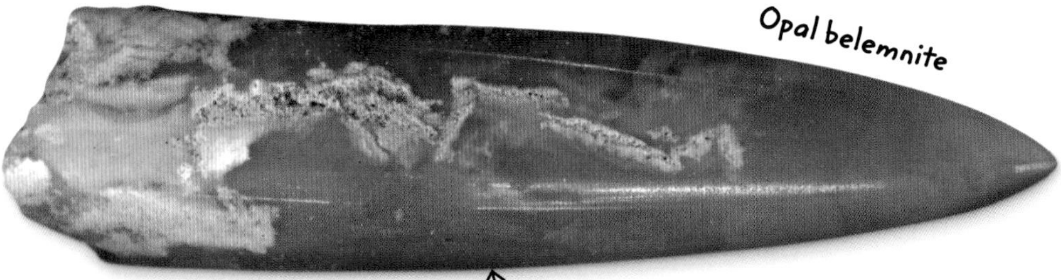

Opal belemnite

Some fossils are preserved as precious gems, like this belemnite made of rainbow-colored opal. Opalized fossils are usually found inside mines in southern Australia.

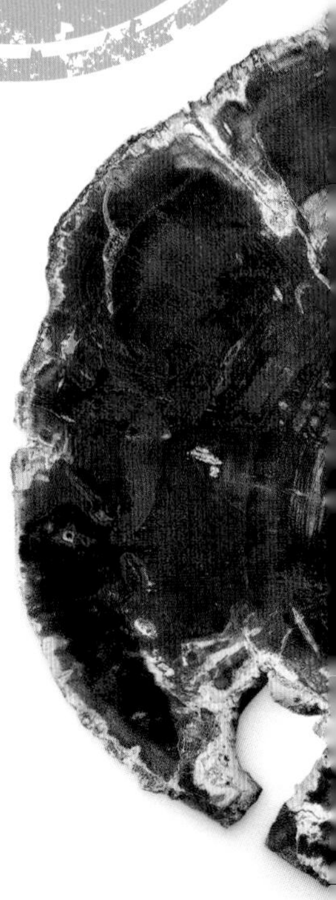

# Hidden treasure

Some fossils look dull on the outside, until they are cut in half and polished. This ammonite is filled with bright minerals, which have preserved details of its internal chambers.

*Ammonite cut in half*

Ammolite is a type of shiny gemstone that is made from the shells of certain kinds of ammonite, mainly found in Alberta, Canada.

Amber is fossilized tree resin. In life, the sticky resin may trap plants and animals, such as this insect. Over time, the resin hardens into golden amber.

*Petrified wood*

**Fly trapped in amber**

Petrified wood can come in a variety of different colors. The color differences depend on the types of minerals that replaced the original wood.

# First fossil finders

Even though fossils have been hiding underground for millions of years, it is only in the last two centuries that scientists have really begun to understand them. The first people to find and name fossils had to figure out what they were.

## Mary Anning
(1799–1847)

English paleontologist Mary was just 12 when she found a huge fossil with her brother. It was an ichthyosaur—one of the earliest discovered. She also uncovered the first plesiosaur.

Ichthyosaurus skull

## Georges Cuvier
(1769–1832)

Georges was a French scientist who compared the bones of animals. He used fossils to prove that species from the past had become extinct, such as the mammothlike mastodons.

Mastodon tooth

The word "dinosaur" was invented in 1842 by paleontologist Richard Owen.

Ancient shark coprolite

# William Buckland
## (1784–1856)

William was an English geologist who studied rocks and named the first dinosaur—Megalosaurus. He also gave coprolites their name, after being given some by Mary Anning.

# Othniel Charles Marsh
## (1831–1899)

American paleontologist Othniel was a rival to Edward Drinker Cope. Othniel named around 80 new species of dinosaurs, including Allosaurus and Triceratops.

Allosaurus skull

# Edward Drinker Cope
## (1840–1897)

Edaphosaurus vertebra with tall spine

Edward was an American paleontologist. He named 56 new species of dinosaurs and hundreds of other ancient animals, such as the mammal ancestor Edaphosaurus.

# The Bone Wars

Othniel and Edward were very competitive in trying to name new prehistoric animals. During these "Bone Wars" some creatures, such as Uintatherium, got named more than once!

Uintatherium

45

# Pycnodus

## (pick-NO-duss)

Pycnodus was a fish that belonged to an extinct, but successful group known as pycnodonts. It was once thought that Pycnodus lived during the Jurassic and Cretaceous periods, but those fossils appear to belong to other pycnodonts.

A cone-shaped plate covered in teeth was present on both the upper and lower jaws of Pycnodus's mouth.

Pycnodus had round, oblong teeth that were used to crush tough food, such as shellfish.

Some teeth were lost during fossilization.

The fossils of another type of ancient fish, Lepidotes (leppy-DOE-tees), have buttonlike, crushing teeth.

A Pycnodus tooth plate looks a lot like corn on the cob!

## Fossil fish

Pycnodus is mostly known from isolated teeth—some of which were found in the stomach of an ancient whale—but many complete skeletons have been discovered. The best fossils come from a site in the village of Bolca, in Italy.

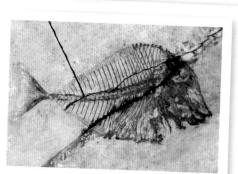

Pycnodus fossil from Bolca, Italy

# Otodus megalodon

## (oh-TOE-dus MEG-a-low-don)

### Fact file

» **Length:** 59 ft (18 m)
» **Diet:** Carnivore
» **Period:** Neogene
» **Location:** Worldwide

Three times larger than a great white shark, this gigantic fish was possibly the deadliest predator ever to have evolved. Megalodons are known almost entirely from thousands of their enormous fossilized teeth.

LARGEST EXTINCT SHARK

Each massive tooth was up to 7 in (18 cm) long. No wonder this species was named "megalodon," which means big tooth!

Serrated edges made the tooth sharp like a steak knife, perfect for tearing through skin, muscle, and fat.

## Shark food

Today's great white sharks look similar to megalodons, but they did not descend from them. In fact, both species lived at the same time, and great white sharks probably even preyed on young megalodons.

**Great white shark fossil tooth**

Megalodons were almost as long as two buses!

The tip of the triangle-shaped tooth was pointed for piercing prey.

47

# Coccosteus
## (cok-oh-STEE-us)

Armored fish were common in the Devonian Period. Coccosteus belonged to one group, called placoderms. Most Coccosteus fossils are of the armor-plated head. However, full skeletons have been found, some with their last meal of fish still inside.

Only the head and front part of the body were covered in bony armor. This protected Coccosteus from predators.

Even the eyes of this fish were surrounded by protective armor plating.

Coccosteus did not have teeth. Instead, it had fanglike plates of bone that were used to slice up prey.

Coccosteus's snapping jawbones formed scissor-like slicing edges that were self-sharpening.

## Placoderm predators

Armored placoderms were some of the earliest fish to evolve jaws. The deadliest of all was the giant Dunkleosteus (DUN-kell-OSS-tee-us), which was the first-ever top marine predator.

Dunkleosteus

# Drepanaspis

## (DREP-an-ASP-iss)

Drepanaspis was an unusual jawless fish with a flattened, pancakelike body that was heavily armored. Many complete fossils have been discovered and most come from a site in Germany, known as the Hunsrück Slate.

**Fact file**

» **Length:** 14 in (35 cm)
» **Diet:** Carnivore
» **Period:** Devonian
» **Location:** Europe

Drepanaspis was shaped like a table-tennis paddle, with a flat body and a narrow tail.

Small eyes were set far apart, which gave a wide view for spotting predators and prey.

Strangely, Drepanaspis's mouth faced up, rather than down. It caught prey near the seafloor.

Thick scales ran along the tail and served as extra protection.

The large, bony head shield served as protection from predators. A flat body would also have made the fish hard to attack from above.

## The Age of Fish

Paleontologists call the Devonian Period the "Age of Fish." During this time in Earth's history, more than 400 million years ago, lots of different types of fish evolved, and some took over the oceans as the dominant predators.

Drepanaspis lived during the Devonian Period.

# Tiktaalik

## (tik-TAA-lick)

During a trip to Arctic Canada in 2004, paleontologists discovered the first Tiktaalik fossils. This strange-looking fish lived in rivers and lakes but had limblike fins capable of pulling itself out of the water.

» **Length:** 10 ft (3 m)
» **Diet:** Carnivore
» **Period:** Devonian
» **Location:** North America

Armlike, bony fins were strong enough to support Tiktaalik's body as it dragged itself onto land.

Tiktaalik had a flat, pointed skull. Its eyes were on top of its head, unlike most fish.

A covering of almost square, overlapping scales covered Tiktaalik's body.

## Fossil fish

Tiktaalik belonged to an ancient group of fish known as lobe-finned fish. One of the most well-known living examples is the coelacanth (SEE-la-canth), which also has limblike fins.

**Modern coelacanth**

A flat, triangular-shaped head is more typical of an amphibian than a fish.

# Eryops

**(EH-ree-ops)**

Amphibians such as Eryops were among the first large vertebrate animals in the fossil record that were capable of living comfortably both in and out of water. It was a top predator in its environment.

**Fact file**

» **Length:** 10 ft (3 m)
» **Diet:** Carnivore
» **Period:** Permian
» **Location:** North America

The tail was strong but short, which suggests Eryops was not a fast or powerful swimmer.

A large, long skull was attached to a very short neck. The name Eryops means "drawn-out face," after its long snout.

Strong legs and feet were capable of supporting the weight of the body on land.

## Early amphibians

Amphibians evolved from fish around 380 million years ago. Leaving the water behind meant they could find new food sources. Some, such as Seymouria (see-MORE-ee-ah), lived mostly on land.

Seymouria fossil

Eryops had sharp teeth—even in the roof of its mouth—to help hold on to slippery fish.

# Echmatemys

## (ECK-mat-eh-MISS)

You can see from this Echmatemys fossil that it was a type of turtle. Its relatives still survive today! This fossil is well-preserved, but more commonly, fossils of just the shell or shell fragments are found.

A tough shell provided protection while on land and in water.

**Turtles are one of the oldest surviving reptile groups.**

Echmatemys could pull its head inside its shell to stay safe from predators.

## Past poop

Fossilized poop is known as coprolite. Many turtle coprolites have been found. We know they belonged to turtles by comparing the shapes and sizes with modern turtle dung!

*Turtle coprolite*

The tail was long and thin and made up of numerous vertebrae (bones from the spine).

Studies of Echmatemys's feet and bones suggest it was not a strong swimmer and spent most of its time out of water.

# Edaphosaurus

## (ed-a-foe-SORE-us)

Edaphosaurus was one of the largest animals of its time. Though it might look a bit like a giant lizard, this herbivore was more closely related to mammals. Its unusual skeleton shows it had a tall sail on its back.

» **Length:** 11 ft (3.5 m)
» **Diet:** Herbivore
» **Period:** Carboniferous to Permian
» **Location:** Europe and North America

Edaphosaurus had large tooth plates filled with round teeth, which helped it to chew tough plants.

A row of tall spines would have supported a large sail in life. Bony spikes stuck out from the sides of the sail.

The thick tail was incredibly long, making up almost half the length of the body.

Jaws containing peglike teeth were used for collecting low-growing plants.

## Reptile or mammal?

Even though Edaphosaurus and its relatives, such as carnivorous Dimetrodon (die-MET-roe-don), were scaly, they were both synapsids. Synapsids are a huge group of animals that includes mammals and their close relatives.

Dimetrodon

# Stenopterygius

## (sten-OP-terr-IDGE-ee-us)

Stenopterygius was one of the most common sea creatures of its time. It belonged to a group of marine reptiles known as ichthyosaurs. Thousands of Stenopterygius fossils have been found, mainly from around the town of Holzmaden, Germany.

Sharply pointed teeth were ideal for snatching fast-moving prey, such as fish and squid.

Only the lower part of the crescent-shaped tail fin, or fluke, contained bones. The fluke was moved in a side-to-side motion to help Stenopterygius swim.

Both the front fins and back fins were used to help steer and change direction in the water.

## Ichthyosaurs

Ichthyosaurs appeared roughly 20 million years before the dinosaurs. Some species had dolphin- or sharklike bodies, whereas others, such as Shonisaurus (SHON-ee-SORE-us), were the size of whales.

Shonisaurus

Fossils reveal the front fin was made up of multiple fingers. Some species had as many as 10 fingers!

54

# Elasmosaurus

## (el-LAZZ-moe-SORE-us)

Elasmosaurus belonged to the plesiosaurs—a family of very varied sea reptiles. It gives its name to a special group of plesiosaurs, the elasmosaurs, which had incredibly long necks. The first Elasmosaurus bones were found in Kansas in 1867.

### Fact file

» **Length:** 39 ft (12 m)
» **Diet:** Carnivore
» **Period:** Cretaceous
» **Location:** North America

Sharp, peglike teeth were ideal for snatching fish from schools or the seafloor.

## Plesiosaurs

Like all reptiles, plesiosaurs breathed air, even though they lived in the sea. Many of them were top predators, but they were wiped out by the asteroid that destroyed the dinosaurs.

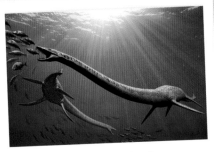

Elasmosaurus feeding

Elasmosaurus had more than 70 vertebrae in its neck! It is one of the longest-necked animals ever to have lived.

Four large flippers were used to swim. They were not strong enough for walking on land—plesiosaurs lived only in the water.

**Elasmosaurus' neck was longer than a giraffe is tall!**

Elasmosaur skulls are rare because they easily become detached from the very long neck during fossilization.

# Scaphognathus

## (ska-fog-NAY-thuss)

Long before birds took to the sky, flying reptiles called pterosaurs dominated the air. Scaphognathus was a hawk-sized pterosaur that lived about 150 million years ago, hunting small animals to eat.

Pterosaurs had wings made of skin, like bats, rather than feathers.

Scaphognathus means "boat jaw," as this pterosaur had a wide mouth.

A long finger bone supported a sheet of leathery skin, which created a wing.

This fossil is embedded in limestone rock and was discovered in Germany.

## Pterosaurs

Pterosaurs existed during the Mesozoic Era. The largest had a wingspan of 36 ft (11 m), but most were smaller, such as Rhamphorhynchus (ram-foh-RINK-uss), which reached 5 ft (1.5 m) across.

Rhamphorhynchus

- » **Wingspan:** 35 in (90 cm)
- » **Diet:** Carnivore
- » **Period:** Jurassic
- » **Location:** Europe

# Platecarpus

## (PLAH-teh-CAR-pus)

This ancient marine reptile belonged to a group called mosasaurs. They lived during the Cretaceous Period and looked a bit like crocodiles with flippers. Platecarpus reached a similar size to the largest saltwater crocodiles.

### Fact file

» **Length:** 23 ft (7 m)
» **Diet:** Carnivore
» **Period:** Cretaceous
» **Location:** Worldwide

Pointed, conical teeth were perfect for gripping slippery fish and tearing apart other big sea reptiles.

A ring of bone surrounded each of Platecarpus's eyes.

Long jaws in a triangle-shaped head were typical of mosasaurs.

## Mosasaurs

The top predators in the Cretaceous ocean were huge mosasaurs, such as Mosasaurus (MOSE-ah-SORE-us), which could reach 50 ft (15 m) in length. A long, powerful tail drove mosasaurs quickly through the water.

Mosasaurus

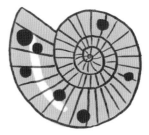

Some ammonite fossils have been found with mosasaur teeth marks on them.

Struthiomimus (STROO-thee-oh-MIME-us) was an ostrichlike dinosaur that lived in North America in the Cretaceous Period. In life, it would have been covered in fluffy feathers.

*Dinosaurs had holes in their skulls, which are different from those in mammals.*

# Dinosaurs

The most famous of all prehistoric animals, dinosaurs dominated the Earth during the Mesozoic Era. This group of reptiles ruled the globe, until an asteroid hit the planet at the end of the Cretaceous Period, wiping out the non-bird dinosaurs.

*All dinosaurs had claws. Some were sharp for slashing, while others were more hooflike for digging.*

*Struthiomimus had long legs that made it a fast runner. Dinosaurs held their legs underneath their bodies, unlike other reptiles.*

## Key dinosaur discoveries

Our knowledge of dinosaurs is improving all the time. Over the last 200 years, fossil discoveries have changed our view of dinosaurs from scaly monsters to a huge variety of intriguing creatures.

*The first dinosaur to be named was Megalosaurus in 1824. The name means "great lizard." It was known from just a few bones, including this lower jaw.*

*Eoraptor was discovered in 1991 and is one of the earliest dinosaur fossils ever found—it is around 230 million years old.*

Dinosaurs had very long hip bones. They came in two different shapes: one birdlike and one lizardlike.

On average, a new species of dinosaur is found every other week!

Most dinosaurs had a long tail to balance their body weight.

## Birds are dinosaurs!

Some dinosaurs, such as Microraptor (MY-crow-RAP-tor), could fly, but they weren't birds. All non-bird dinosaurs died out when the asteroid hit. However, one group of smaller, feathered dinosaurs survived, and they are today's birds.

**Microraptor**

Sinosauropteryx was the first non-bird dinosaur discovered with feathers. We even know that it was red and white with a striped tail.

# Stegosaurus

## (STEG-oh-SORE-us)

When the first Stegosaurus fossil was unearthed in the 1870s, it was thought to be an animal related to plesiosaurs and turtles! However, Stegosaurus was actually the largest member of the stegosaur family of dinosaurs.

» **Length:** 30 ft (9 m)
» **Diet:** Herbivore
» **Period:** Jurassic
» **Location:** Europe and North America

Despite its bulky body, Stegosaurus's brain was only about the size of a plum.

Stegosaurus used its diamond-shaped teeth to chew plants.

Four massive, bony spikes were a fierce weapon against predators.

Two rows of big, bony plates were embedded in the skin along the back and not attached to the skeleton.

When Stegosaurus was first reconstructed, scientists thought its plates laid flat along its back.

## Colorful plates

The plates on the back of Stegosaurus were probably brightly colored in life. It is thought they were mainly used for display, to show off and attract mates, but also to scare away predators.

Stegosaurus

# Euoplocephalus

**(YOU-owe-plo-SEFF-ah-lus)**

Heavily-armored Euoplocephalus was a tanklike dinosaur that belonged to the ankylosaur group. Dozens of skulls and skeletons of this animal have been found since it was first discovered in 1897.

Rows of thick, and sometimes pointed, bony lumps made up part of a large shield on this dinosaur's back.

A massive club at the end of the tail was used as a bone-shattering, defensive weapon.

The tail club may have been swung at speeds of up to 70 mph (110 kph).

Each foot had hooflike claws that were used for digging in the ground.

The triangular skull ended in a rounded beak that was used to collect plants to eat.

*Nodosaur*

*Ankylosaur*

Ankylosaurs and nodosaurs looked very similar, but nodosaurs didn't have a club at the end of their tails.

## Bony shield

Ankylosaurs and their relatives, the nodosaurs, had massive coats of bony body armor that protected their necks, backs, and tails. The nodosaur Polacanthus (pole-a-KAN-thuss) had an extra shield over its hips.

*Polacanthus*

# Ornithopods
## (OR-nith-oh-pods)

Ornithopods were a group of plant-eating dinosaurs, and their fossils have been found all around the world. The first ornithopods were turkey-sized, but over millions of years they evolved into bulky giants—some of which were longer than a shipping container.

## Hypsilophodon
## (HIP-sih-LOAF-oh-don)

Hypsilophodon is one of the best preserved dinosaurs found in the UK. The first bones were discovered in 1849, but were mistakenly thought to be of a young Iguanodon.

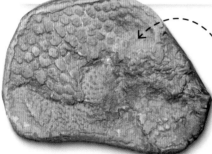

This fossil shows the dinosaur's skin, which was formed when it was pressed into soft mud.

## Edmontosaurus
## (ed-MONT-oh-SORE-us)

Edmontosaurus was one of the largest and last-surviving ornithopods. This is known from many fossils, including some with mummified skin.

Some ornithopods could switch between walking on four legs or two.

A giant, bony thumb spike was probably used to grab plants and help the dinosaur defend itself. 

# Iguanodon
## (ig-GWAH-no-don)

Iguanodon was a huge ornithopod that weighed as much as an African elephant. In 1878, an incredible discovery of more than 30 Iguanodon fossils was made inside a coal mine in Belgium.

# Parasaurolophus
## (PA-ra-SORE-oh-LOAF-us)

Parasaurolophus belonged to a group of ornithopods named hadrosaurs, often called "duck-bills." Their long jaws were filled with rows of teeth that were constantly replaced.

The long, hollow head crest may have helped the dinosaur to make loud sounds.

The enlarged, hollow crest on the snout may have grown larger over time as the animal aged.

The most commonly found Hypsilophodon fossils are tail vertebrae.

# Muttaburrasaurus
## (MOO-tah-BUH-ruh-SORE-us)

The first Muttaburrasaurus skeleton was discovered in 1963 near Muttaburra, Australia. It is one of the most complete dinosaurs found in Australia.

# Patagotitan

## (pat-AG-oh-tie-tan)

**Fact file**

» **Length:** 102 ft (31 m)
» **Diet:** Herbivore
» **Period:** Cretaceous
» **Location:** South America

In 2010, a farmer discovered parts of a gigantic dinosaur on a farm in an area of Argentina called Patagonia. Paleontologists excavated the site and revealed one of the largest dinosaurs ever, which was named Patagotitan.

Patagotitan would have dined on giant trees, such as Araucaria.

This is the right femur (thigh bone) of Patagotitan. The pointed end is where the femur slotted into the hip.

**Patagotitan's femur alone was around 8 ft (2.4 m) long!**

## Giant dinosaurs

The largest animals ever to walk the Earth were the sauropod dinosaurs, which had tremendously long necks and tails. The biggest of these were the titanosaurs, such as Argentinosaurus (ARE-jen-TEEN-oh-SORE-us) and Patagotitan.

Paleontologists can estimate the size of Patagotitan by studying bones like the femur.

More than 130 bones like this one were discovered at the dig site and belonged to at least six individuals.

Argentinosaurus

# Khaan

## (KAHN)

Khaan was a birdlike dinosaur known from fossils collected in the Gobi Desert in eastern Asia. An incredible discovery was made of a pair of skeletons found only 8 in (20 cm) apart, which likely died at the same time.

### Fact file

» **Length:** 6 ft (1.8 m)
» **Diet:** Carnivore
» **Period:** Cretaceous
» **Location:** Asia

Large claws on the feet were used for digging and defense—to kick at predators.

The upper and lower jaws were toothless. A large, powerful beak was used for feeding.

The long neck and tail were pulled backward when the animal decayed. This posture is called a "death pose."

## Caring parents

Some of Khaan's relatives, including the emu-sized Citipati (SIH-tee-PAH-tee), have been discovered sitting on clutches of eggs. This suggests they looked after their eggs and young.

Citipati

Many eggs have been found from cousins of Khaan, such as this Oviraptor (OVE-ee-rap-tor) egg.

# Triceratops

## (try-SERRA-tops)

Triceratops was among the largest and very last of the horned dinosaurs. When the first fossil was discovered in 1887 in Colorado, it was mistakenly thought to have been an ancient bison because of its large horns.

Triceratops was huge. It would have weighed four times as much as a modern rhinoceros.

Gigantic brow horns measured up to 3 ft (1 m) long. They were used for battling with other Triceratops and predators.

A large, powerful beak was used to grasp and snap tough plants, which were then chewed up by many teeth in the jaws.

## Giant frills

A huge, bony frill protected Triceratops' head and neck. However, it was also used for display to attract mates. The frill would have been covered with scaly skin, and it was possibly brightly colored.

Triceratops

Triceratops was twice as long as the average car.

66

# Stegoceras

## (steh-goh-SEH-rass)

Stegoceras was a goat-sized member of the pachycephalosaur group of dinosaurs, which are known for having thick, bony skulls. Most Stegoceras fossils are of its tough, bony skull dome.

### Fact file

» **Length:** 6¹/₂ ft (2 m)
» **Diet:** Herbivore
» **Period:** Cretaceous
» **Location:** North America

The thick, dome-shaped skull was made of solid bone that could withstand heavy force.

Stegoceras' bony skull was up to 4 in (9 cm) thick!

Many small teeth filled the jaws. Stegoceras probably ate a variety of plants, as well as seeds and fruits.

Bony bumps and spikes surrounded the dome.

## Head to head

Pachycephalosaurs, such as Stegoceras and its larger cousin, Pachycephalosaurus (PACK-ee-SEF-a-low-SORE-us), took part in headbutting and side-ramming contests. Fossils show their domes became bashed and dented from this.

Pachycephalosauruses clash

# Tyrannosaurus

## (TIE-ran-oh-SORE-us)

» **Length:** 43 ft (13 m)
» **Diet:** Carnivore
» **Period:** Cretaceous
» **Location:** North America

The first fossil of Tyrannosaurus rex, or T. rex, was found in Montana more than 100 years ago. Skeletons of at least 50 T. rex have been found since, some almost complete, and one with preserved, scaly skin.

Over 50 teeth lined T. rex's giant jaws. Some were as big as bananas and could crunch through bone.

A long tail helped to balance this dinosaur's large and heavy head.

A second set of ribs, called gastralia, probably helped with breathing.

The short arms had a pair of curved claws at the end that may have been used to hold struggling prey.

T. rex weighed as much as 8 tons (7 metric tons), almost twice as heavy as the average African elephant!

## Superior predator

T. rex is believed to be one of the deadliest dinosaurs. This mighty meat-eater was at the top of the food chain. It had excellent vision, sensational smell, and the most powerful bite of any animal that ever lived.

Tyrannosaurus chasing a Triceratops

Several Tyrannosaurus skulls have been found. The largest is over 5 ft (1.5 m) long.

# Velociraptor

## (vel-OSS-ee-RAP-tor)

Velociraptor is one of the most famous dinosaurs. Its fossils were first found in 1923, as part of an expedition to the Gobi Desert in Asia. At least 10 almost-whole skeletons have been found in Mongolia and China.

### Fact file

» **Length:** 6½ ft (2 m)
» **Diet:** Carnivore
» **Period:** Cretaceous
» **Location:** Asia

Large eye sockets show us Velociraptor had big eyes, perfect for spotting prey even at night.

The skull is long and slender and measures around 10 in (25 cm).

A large "killer claw" on each of Velociraptor's feet helped it to pin down and slash at prey.

As many as 60 sharp, serrated teeth in Velociraptor's jaws were used to slice through flesh.

## Desert habitat

Turkey-sized Velociraptor lived in dry and sandy deserts similar to the Gobi Desert today. It was hot by day and chilly by night, and Velociraptor's feathers helped it stay warm when it was cold outside.

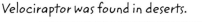

Velociraptor was found in deserts.

69

# Archaeopteryx

## (ar-kee-OP-ter-ix)

**Fact file**

» **Length:** 20 in (50 cm)
» **Diet:** Carnivore
» **Period:** Jurassic
» **Location:** Europe

Archaeopteryx was the first dinosaur to show a link between birds and reptiles. This fossil was collected in Germany in the 1870s, and it is the first nearly complete Archaeopteryx ever discovered. It was found by a farmer who sold it to buy a cow!

Sharp claws on its wings suggest that Archaeopteryx climbed up trees.

Archaeopteryx fossils have been found with feathers and birdlike wings.

The long, bony tail was covered in feathers. It was used for balance when gliding from treetops.

Common magpie

## Feather colors

Paleontologists have observed fossilized color pigments in the feathers of Archaeopteryx. One study found that it probably had black and white feathers, similar to a common magpie.

This Archaeopteryx skull shows its sharp, pointed teeth, which were used to hold prey.

# Confuciusornis

## (con-FEW-shus-OR-niss)

The first fossils of this crow-sized bird were found in 1995. Since then, several thousand specimens have been found in northeastern China. The fossils are so well preserved that they often contain feathers and skin.

Confuciusornis had a strong, toothless beak. Originally, it was believed to be a herbivore, but one fossil contained fish remains inside. ---

One Confuciusornis was found inside the stomach of a dinosaur!

Confuciusornis was a good flier and had a wingspan of about 28 in (70 cm).

This bird had four long toes, one of which pointed backward. This suggests it perched in trees.

## Tail feathers

There are two different types of Confuciusornis fossil: the first with two very long tail feathers, and the second with no tail feathers at all. Scientists think the fossils with long tail feathers were males, and those without, females.

Male Confuciusornis

# Dinornis

## (die-NOR-niss)

Ostrichlike Dinornis was the largest member of a group of large, flightless birds called moa. They lived in New Zealand until just over 500 years ago, when the last of them were hunted to extinction by humans.

Fact file

» **Height:** 12 ft (3.6 m)
» **Diet:** Herbivore
» **Period:** Quaternary
» **Location:** Oceania

A sharp beak was used to pluck fruits, shoots, and seeds.

Lots of plant remains have been found inside the stomach of Dinornis.

The long, flexible neck gave Dinornis an advantage over other herbivores when reaching up high for food.

## Haast's eagle

Haast's eagle lived in New Zealand at the same time as moa, even hunting them. With a wingspan of up to 10 ft (3 m), it is the largest eagle to have ever lived.

Long, powerful legs made Dinornis a fast runner.

Moa were the only birds without wings, although their bodies were covered in feathers.

Moa were the largest herbivores in New Zealand for millions of years.

Haast's eagle attacking a moa

# Dorudon

## (DO-roo-don)

Dorudon was a type of toothed whale, like a dolphin. Its fossils help to show how whales evolved from land-living mammals—unlike a whale today, it still had small back legs! The first fossils were studied in 1845.

» **Length:** 16 ft (5 m)
» **Diet:** Carnivore
» **Period:** Paleogene
» **Location:** Worldwide

Dorudon's back legs were "vestigial," meaning that they were no longer used. Dorudon lived entirely in the water.

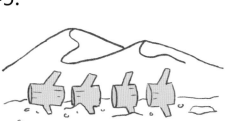

Many Dorudon fossils have been found in Egypt at a desert site called Wadi Al-Hitan, which means "Valley of the Whales."

A narrow skull suggests that Dorudon dined primarily on fish. However, it probably also ate other sea mammals.

Paddlelike forelimbs were used for steering. The tail was moved up and down to push Dorudon through the water.

## Watch out!

The first gigantic whale to evolve was Basilosaurus (ba-SILL-oh-SORE-us), which was as long as 59 ft (18 m). This giant, which also had small back legs, lived alongside Dorudon, which it hunted.

*Basilosaurus swimming*

Some of the teeth were bladelike and gave Dorudon its name, which means "spear tooth."

73

# Prehistoric world

One of the most fascinating things about fossils is that they allow us to re-create what ancient Earth looked like. Artists can use their knowledge of modern plants and animals as well as scientific information to bring the prehistoric world to life.

Utahraptor was a top predator in its habitat. Although not found with feather fossils, it was probably feathered like its close relatives.

This reconstruction shows an area of Utah in the Cretaceous Period. Ferns carpeted the ground and would have been food for herbivores, such as the nodosaur Gastonia.

This area was covered in rivers and lakes in the Cretaceous. Fossils of fish and even small sharks have been found.

# Reconstructing the past

By studying all the fossils and rocks in one area, we can tell what the environment was like millions of years ago. The hills of the Cedar Mountain Formation in the western United States were formed during the Cretaceous Period.

Cedar Mountain Formation today

Many of the rocks from the Cedar Mountain Formation in Utah and Colorado are sedimentary. Sandstone and mudstone are common.

Only parts of Utahraptor have so far been found as fossils. It belonged to the same family as Velociraptor and could grow up to 23 ft (7 m) long.

This fossil shell belonged to Glyptops, an ancient turtle that lived at the same time as Utahraptor. It swam in freshwater lakes and ponds.

Forests covered the land where Utahraptor lived. During the wet season, the ground was flooded with water.

75

# Morganucodon

## (MORE-gan-oo-CODE-on)

Shrewlike Morganucodon is one of the earliest mammals, or at least a close relative of mammals. Thousands of bones and teeth belonging to Morganucodon have been found, mostly inside quarries and caves, especially in Wales.

Morganucodon's jaws were strong and capable of crunching up tough prey, such as beetles.

Sharp teeth suggest this animal was a predator—but only of insects. It may have hunted at night.

Morganucodon weighed just over ½ oz (18 g)—that's less than a house mouse.

## Early mammals

Mammals appeared during the Triassic Period. The earliest species, such as Megazostrodon (MEG-ah-ZO-stroh-don), were small and lived in burrows or in trees to keep from becoming dinner for dinosaurs.

Megazostrodon

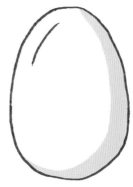

Morganucodon probably laid leathery-shelled eggs like a modern platypus or echidna.

# Gomphotherium

**(GOM-foe-THEE-ree-um)**

Gomphotherium, meaning "welded beast," was named after its long, straight tusks. It belonged to a group of elephant relatives known as gomphotheres. They had four tusks, and some species were as large as African elephants.

**Fact file**

» **Length:** 16 ft (5 m)
» **Diet:** Herbivore
» **Period:** Neogene
» **Location:** Africa, Asia, Europe, and North America

Gomphotherium had a large hump just above its shoulders.

Long upper tusks were used for digging, display, and defense against predators and other gomphotheres.

The tusks in the lower jaw were shorter and used for digging up food and stripping bark from trees.

Gomphotherium had a very short tail.

## Herd behavior

Discoveries of gomphothere fossils found together show that they probably lived in herds, like modern elephants. This may be partly why they were so successful.

Gomphotherium herd

Strong molar teeth were used to grind up a variety of plants—mainly grasses.

# Ursus spelaeus

## (ER-suss SPEE-lee-uss)

The mighty Ursus spelaeus is also known as the cave bear. This bear was a common sight in Ice Age Europe, where it lived alongside early humans. It may have competed with humans for the best caves.

» **Length:** 11 ft (3.5 m)
» **Diet:** Omnivore
» **Period:** Quaternary
» **Location:** Europe

The cave bear had a large skull. The largest bears weighed perhaps as much as 1 ton (1 metric ton).

Big canine teeth were used for biting and tearing up prey.

Thousands of fossils, just like this skull, have been found deep inside caves.

Mother brown bear and her cubs

## Brown bear

The cave bear is an extinct relative of the living brown bear and would have looked very similar. Brown bears only use caves occasionally, but cave bears appear to have spent much of their lives inside caves.

Flat cheek teeth were used to grind tough leaves, fruits, and seeds.

# Coelodonta

## (SEE-low-DON-tah)

There are several types of the extinct rhino Coelodonta, including one of the most famous Ice Age mammals—the woolly rhinoceros. Some very rare fossils have been discovered frozen in ice with their organs still inside.

» **Length:** 13 ft (4 m)
» **Diet:** Herbivore
» **Period:** Neogene to Quaternary
» **Location:** Asia and Europe

Coelodonta had two horns. The front horn could be more than 3 ft (1 m) long and was used as a weapon against predators and competitors.

Some woolly rhinoceroses lived in icy areas. To combat the freezing cold, they had a thick coat of hair.

## Cave paintings

Artworks created by early humans often show the animals they lived alongside. Some of these paintings, such as this one, show illustrations of Coelodonta that were painted over 30,000 years ago!

Cave painting of a woolly rhinoceros

Large molar teeth were ideal for grazing on grasses and other plants. Some fossil plants have even been found stuck inside the teeth!

# Smilodon

## (SMILE-oh-don)

This big cat was a top predator that caught its prey by ambush. Thousands of Smilodon fossils have been discovered. Most of them, such as this skeleton, come from a site called the La Brea Tar Pits in California.

» **Length:** 6½ ft (2 m)
» **Diet:** Carnivore
» **Period:** Quaternary
» **Location:** North America and South America

Unlike modern big cats, Smilodon had a short tail.

Studies of bones in the throat, called hyoids, suggest that Smilodon had a fearsome roar, like a lion's.

Smilodon used its strong, powerful, and muscular body to pin down prey and fight rivals.

## Sticky tar

The La Brea Tar Pits fossil site is filled with lakes of a sticky black substance called tar. The tar was a natural trap—animals caught in the gooey liquid attracted predators, such as Smilodon, which then also got stuck!

La Brea Tar Pits

Smilodon had huge canine teeth, which could grow up to 10 in (25 cm) long.

# Mammuthus

## (MA-muh-thuss)

Mammuthus was one of the largest land mammals ever to have lived. Also known as mammoths, the fossilized remains of these animals have been found inside caves, quarries, and even frozen in ice.

Fact file

» **Length:** 13 ft (4 m)
» **Diet:** Herbivore
» **Period:** Quaternary
» **Location:** Africa, Asia, Europe, and North America

Early humans used the large bones of Mammuthus to build huts and make tools.

Enormous tusks were used for digging, moving objects, and fighting.

Just like modern-day elephants, Mammuthus had strong and sturdy legs that supported its heavy weight.

## Mammoth molar

Mammoths had six sets of grinding teeth in their lifetime. As a tooth began to wear down, a new tooth grew behind it, which eventually pushed out and replaced the old, worn-out tooth.

**Woolly mammoth tooth**

One type of Mammuthus was the woolly mammoth, which had a hairy coat and lived in icy conditions.

# Mylodon

**(MY-low-don)**

Ground sloths, such as Mylodon, were the huge cousins of modern sloths. The first fossils were found by Charles Darwin, in 1832, in Argentina, and named Mylodon darwinii in his honor. Amazingly, pieces of Mylodon's fur and skin have been discovered.

Mummified Mylodon skin and fur show it had a thick coat of either light- or dark-brown hair.

Mylodon bones, poop, and fur have all been found preserved inside caves.

Some Mylodon skin had bony studs embedded underneath it. These acted as armor against predators.

## Ground sloths

Unlike sloths today, ground sloths did not live in trees or move extremely slowly. Ground sloths, such as Megatherium (MEG-ah-THEER-ee-um), were also much bigger—weighing up to 1,200 times more!

Megatherium

Mylodon's long, sharp claws were used for grasping leaves in trees and for digging.

# Australopithecus

## (OSS-tra-low-PITH-ee-cuss)

Australopithecus was an early human relative that walked upright on two legs. It had a mixture of apelike and humanlike features. The most famous fossil find was made in 1974 in Ethiopia of a young female, nicknamed Lucy.

**Fact file**

» **Height:** 5 ft (1.4 m)
» **Diet:** Omnivore
» **Period:** Neogene
» **Location:** Africa

Australopithecus may have made stone tools, such as this hand ax.

Paleontologists can use fossil skulls to tell what Australopithecus would have looked like in life.

## Fossil footprints

A trail of footprints made by early human relatives— possibly Australopithecus— were discovered at a site called Laetoli in Tanzania. They are nearly 3.7 million years old!

Trail of Laetoli footprints

Only parts of the skull have been found. The lighter portions show the original bones, and the darker parts are reconstructed.

Strong molars show that Australopithecus ate tough plants. Grasses, leaves, and fruits were all on the menu.

# Excavation

Once a fossil is found, it needs to be carefully freed from the surrounding rock so it can be studied. It can take weeks, months, or even years to unearth all the fossils at a dig site.

Paleontologists don't always know what animal they are excavating.

## Finding fossils

In some places where rocks naturally erode, such as at the beach, you may be able to see fossils lying on the ground. However, most fossils are hidden underground and need to be dug out, or excavated.

Edmontosaurus foot

These Edmontosaurus bones are stuck in a bed of rock.

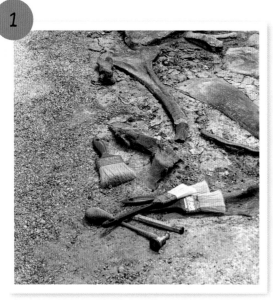

Various tools are used to chip away the rock around the bones. The work is done carefully, so not to damage them. Paleontologists search the whole site to ensure they find all the fossils.

If a larger bone is unearthed, it is wrapped in a jacket of plaster to keep it safe. It can then be transported without damaging it. The fossils will be sent to a laboratory to be studied.

Electric drills and other tools are used to carefully separate the final pieces of rock.

**3**

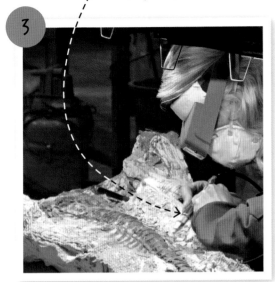

**4**

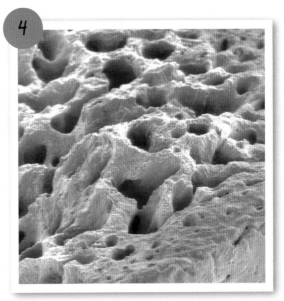

In a lab, smaller tools are used to remove any last pieces of rock, and the bones can be cleaned. Any finds are carefully recorded and described—it may be a new species!

Once the bones are prepared, they can be examined more closely. They may be scanned, or viewed under a microscope—this is a hugely magnified image of a fossil bone.

Wires and supports need to be added to the bones to hold them in place.

Reconstructed Edmontosaurus

## Finished skeleton

Once all the bones have been cleaned and studied, the animal can be reconstructed. Often, some bones will be missing, and models can be used to fill in the gaps.

Artists can use reconstructed skeletons to create 3-D models of prehistoric animals to imagine what they might have looked like in life.

3-D model

# Recent discoveries

We are living through an exciting time for fossil discoveries. New fossils from all over the world are found every day. In recent years, some spectacular fossils have been found, and they have changed the way we think about the past.

In 2020, Kylinxia was discovered in China. This shrimplike arthropod is from the Cambrian Period and has helped scientists to better understand how arthropods evolved.

Kylinxia had five eyes

Australotitan

Australotitan was a giant titanosaur. It is the largest dinosaur found in Australia so far. It was named in 2021 from bones, including this upper arm bone.

## Jurassic seabed

An enormous rocky seabed containing marine animals from the Jurassic, including crinoids and sea urchins, was found in the UK in 2021. The discovery shows a whole ecosystem of animals fossilized together.

Crinoids in rock

Since 2015, four mummified cave lion cubs have been found frozen in thick ice in Russia. They are still covered in soft fur.

Cave lion cubs

Many new types of ceratopsian dinosaur have been found recently, including Regaliceratops from Canada. This dinosaur was named in 2015 and has a crownlike frill.

Regaliceratops

# Regaliceratops means "royal horned face."

## Rediscovered

The Wollemi pine is a tree known from fossils, and it was thought to be extinct. However, in 1994, living examples were discovered near Sydney, Australia. It may have survived since the Cretaceous Period!

Wollemi pine

# Future fossils

Only a tiny percentage of living species on Earth today will be fossilized. To even stand a chance of becoming a fossil, animals and plants must live in specific environments that could eventually lead to them being preserved forever.

Feather

In certain conditions, this kingfisher feather could become a fossil. Buried soo enough and in the right sediments, even the original colors might be retained.

Shell buried

## The right conditions

Many fossils are found in rocks from ancient marshes, riverbeds, and deep oceans—places where life-forms are often buried quickly after dying. Organisms living in these settings today have a greater chance of turning into a fossil in the future.

Snail shell

The hard shells of animals, including snails, have a higher chance of becoming fossilized than soft-bodied creatures, such as worms.

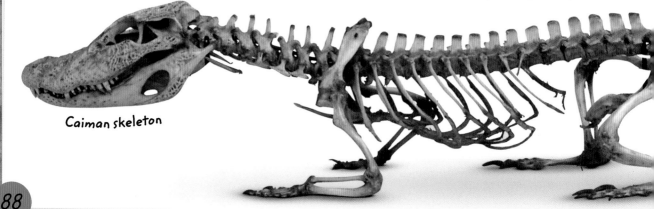

Caiman skeleton

## Future discoveries

Humans may affect what fossils are discovered in the future. Many kinds of animals and plants have been moved around the world, or farmed. Future paleontologists might think that brown rats were found naturally across the globe, or that chickens were one of the most successful animals!

Chickens feeding

Shark teeth

Sharks constantly replace their teeth throughout their lives. This means there is a greater chance that some of these teeth will be found as fossils.

Pine cones

Fossils are a record of life on Earth—but not all species become fossilized.

Remains of trees and wood may be buried completely in swampy areas that could preserve entire forests.

Bones and teeth of animals such as this caiman may be the only parts left behind to become fossils.

# All together

This book shows off just some of the millions of plant and animal fossils that have been discovered. Here you'll find a selection of the organisms shown in the book, and how to say their names.

**Stromatolite**
(stroh-MAT-oh-lite)
pg. 18

**Cooksonia**
(COOK-so-NEE-ah)
pg. 19

**Zamites**
(za-MY-teez)
pg. 20

**Pecopteris**
(peh-KOP-ter-is)
pg. 21

**Lepidodendron**
(leppy-doe-DEN-dron)
pg. 22

**Porana**
(por-AH-na)
pg. 23

**Woodocrinus**
(wood-oh-KRY-nuss)
pg. 24

**Rhizopoterion**
(RY-zo-po-TEH-ree-on)
pg. 25

**Thecosmilia**
(thee-koh-SMILE-ee-a)
pg. 26

**Pygurus**
(PY-gur-uss)
pg. 27

**Didymograptus**
(did-ee-moh-GRAP-tuss)
pg. 28

**Tibia**
(TIB-ee-a)
pg. 29

**Hallucigenia**
(ha-lucy-JEAN-ee-a)
pg. 30

**Tullimonstrum**
(tull-ee-MON-strum)
pg. 31

**Isotelus**
(eye-so-TELL-us)
pg. 32

**Erbenochile**
(er-BEN-oh-CHILL-ee)
pg. 32

**Asaphus**
(A-sa-fuss)
pg. 33

**Walliserops**
(WALL-ee-SERR-ops)
pg. 33

**Triarthrus**
(try-ARTH-russ)
pg. 33

**Pterygotus**
(terry-GOAT-us)
pg. 34

**Archimedes**
(ark-i-MEE-deez)
pg. 35

**Aviculopecten**
(a-VIK-you-low-PECK-ten)
pg. 36

**Meganeura**
(MEGA-new-ra)
pg. 37

**Cyrtospirifer**
(ser-toh-SPIH-rih-fer)
pg. 38

**Cylindroteuthis**
(si-lin-droh-TOO-thiss)
pg. 39

**Nipponites**
(NIP-oh-nites)
pg. 40

**Dactylioceras**
(DACK-till-ee-oh-SAIR-us)
pg. 40

**Ancyloceras**
(an-see-low-SAIR-us)
pg. 41

**Crioceratites**
(kree-oh-sair-a-TITES)
pg. 41

**Kosmoceras**
(koz-moh-SAIR-us)
pg. 41

**Pycnodus**
(pick-NO-duss)
pg. 46

**Otodus megalodon**
(oh-TOE-dus MEG-a-low-don)
pg. 47

**Coccosteus**
(cok-oh-STEE-us)
pg. 48

**Drepanaspis**
(DREP-an-ASP-iss)
pg. 49

**Tiktaalik**
(tik-TAA-lick)
pg. 50

**Eryops**
(EH-ree-ops)
pg. 51

**Echmatemys**
(ECK-mat-eh-MISS)
pg. 52

**Edaphosaurus**
(ed-a-foe-SORE-us)
pg. 53

**Stenopterygius**
(sten-OP-terr-IDGE-ee-us)
pg. 54

**Elasmosaurus**
(el-LAZZ-moe-SORE-us)
pg. 55

**Scaphognathus**
(ska-fog-NAY-thuss)
pg. 56

**Platecarpus**
(PLAH-teh-CAR-pus)
pg. 57

**Stegosaurus**
(STEG-oh-SORE-us)
pg. 60

**Euoplocephalus**
(YOU-owe-plo-SEFF-ah-lus)
pg. 61

**Hypsilophodon**
(HIP-sih-LOAF-oh-don)
pg. 62

**Edmontosaurus**
(ed-MONT-oh-SORE-us)
pg. 62

**Iguanodon**
(ig-GWAH-no-don)
pg. 63

**Parasaurolophus**
(PA-ra-SORE-oh-LOAF-us)
pg. 63

**Muttaburrasaurus**
(MOO-tah-BUH-ruh-SORE-us)
pg. 63

**Patagotitan**
(pat-AG-oh-tie-tan)
pg. 64

**Khaan**
(KAHN)
pg. 65

**Triceratops**
(try-SERRA-tops)
pg. 66

**Stegoceras**
(steh-goh-SEH-rass)
pg. 67

**Tyrannosaurus**
(TIE-ran-oh-SORE-us)
pg. 68

**Velociraptor**
(vel-OSS-ee-RAP-tor)
pg. 69

**Archaeopteryx**
(ar-kee-OP-ter-ix)
pg. 70

**Confuciusornis**
(con-FEW-shus-OR-niss)
pg. 71

**Dinornis**
(die-NOR-niss)
pg. 72

**Dorudon**
(DO-roo-don)
pg. 73

**Morganucodon**
(MORE-gan-oo-CODE-on)
pg. 76

**Gomphotherium**
(GOM-foe-THEE-ree-um)
pg. 77

**Ursus spelaeus**
(ER-suss SPEE-lee-uss)
pg. 78

**Coelodonta**
(SEE-low-DON-tah)
pg. 79

**Smilodon**
(SMILE-oh-don)
pg. 80

**Mammuthus**
(MA-muh-thuss)
pg. 81

**Mylodon**
(MY-low-don)
pg. 82

**Australopithecus**
(OSS-tra-low-PITH-ee-cuss)
pg. 83

# Glossary

### amber
fossilized tree resin. It is a see-through, orange-colored gemstone and can contain the remains of plants and animals from millions of years ago

### ambush
surprise attack

### ammonite
type of marine invertebrate with a shell that is usually spiral-shaped. Related to squid and octopuses, ammonites thrived throughout the Mesozoic Era

### amphibian
cold-blooded vertebrate that is able to live both on land and in water, such as a frog

### antenna
feeler on the heads of arthropods, used to sense the environment

### arthropod
invertebrate with a hard outer skeleton and a segmented body, such as an insect

### belemnite
type of marine invertebrate with a body like a squid. Fossils of belemnites' internal skeletons are common

### bird
warm-blooded vertebrate with feathers and a beak that lays hard-shelled eggs, such as an eagle or owl. Birds are dinosaurs

### carnivore
animal that eats other animals for food; also called a meat-eater

### coprolite
fossilized dung. It can contain traces of an animal's last meal

### crinoid
marine invertebrate that filters food from the water with feathery arms. Crinoids are related to sea urchins and sea stars

### dinosaur
type of reptile that appeared in the Triassic Period and held its legs directly beneath its body. Dinosaurs exist today as birds

### era
named portion of geological time containing lots of different periods

### erosion
process by which rocks are broken down by natural forces, such as wind and rain

### evolution
process whereby one species gives rise to another over many generations

### excavation
process of removing fossils from the ground

### extinction
dying out of a species, which may happen for different reasons, such as hunting or habitat loss

### fish
cold-blooded vertebrate that lives in water and breathes using gills, such as a shark

### fossil
remains or traces of a prehistoric organism. Fossils are usually made of rock

### fossilization
process of an organism transforming into a fossil. Fossilization takes thousands to millions of years

### graptolite
type of marine invertebrate that lives in colonies and filters food from the water

### herbivore
animal that only eats vegetation; also called a plant-eater

## ichthyosaur

type of marine reptile, some of which resembled dolphins. Ichthyosaurs lived during the Mesozoic Era

## invertebrate

animal without a backbone

## mammal

warm-blooded, hairy vertebrate that produces milk to feed its young; cats and dogs are mammals

## mineral

substance made from a mix of chemical elements that usually forms sharp-edged crystals

## mosasaur

type of marine reptile with a large head and flippers. Mosasaurs existed during the Cretaceous Period

## mummified

description of a preserved life-form that still has evidence of its soft parts, such as skin and scales

## omnivore

animal that eats both other animals and plants

## organism

life-form

## paleontologist

scientist who studies the history of life on Earth, usually through the examination of fossils

## period

named portion of geological time. Multiple periods make up an era

## pigment

natural material that gives an animal or plant its color

## plesiosaur

type of marine reptile that varied in appearance, including pliosaurs, which had giant heads with big teeth, and elasmosaurs, which had extremely long necks

## pollination

transfer of pollen from one flower to another, so that seeds can be produced. A pollinator is an animal that carries the pollen

## predator

animal that hunts other animals for food

## prehistoric

description of a species that existed before written history

## preservation

keeping something the same, or preventing it from being damaged or destroyed

## prey

animal that is hunted and killed by another animal for food

## pterosaur

type of flying reptile with leathery wings. Pterosaurs lived throughout the Mesozoic Era and were the first vertebrates capable of flight

## reconstruct

rebuild the body or skeleton of a plant or animal from its fossils

## reptile

cold-blooded, scaly vertebrate, such as a crocodile, snake, or turtle. Reptiles usually lay soft-shelled eggs on land

## rock

substance made from a mix of minerals. There are three types of rock: igneous, sedimentary, and metamorphic

## species

type of organism, such as a plant or animal, that can only usually reproduce with members of the same species

## spore

reproductive cell produced by some plants, fungi, and lichens

## trilobite

type of marine arthropod with a body divided into three sections

## vertebra

backbone

## vertebrate

animal with an internal bony or cartilaginous skeleton, including a skull and backbone

# Index

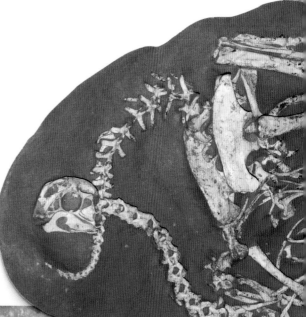

# Acknowledgments

Dean Lomax would like to thank Natalie Turner for reviewing early drafts of this book. He would also like to thank fellow paleontologist and friend, Nigel Larkin, who has made remarkable contributions to paleontology—long may their adventures continue.

DK would like to thank Kathleen Teece and Kieran Jones for editorial assistance, Bettina Myklebust Stovne for illustration, Polly Goodman for proofreading, and Helen Peters for the index.

**The publisher would like to thank the following for their kind permission to reproduce their photographs:**

**(Key: a-above; b-below/bottom; c-center; f-far; l-left; r-right; t-top)**

**1 Alamy Stock Photo:** Bill Gozansky (Background); Martin Shields (c). **2 Alamy Stock Photo:** The Natural History Museum, London (tc). **Dorling Kindersley:** Natural History Museum, London (bc). **2–3 Alamy Stock Photo:** Bill Gozansky (Background). **3 Alamy Stock Photo:** Roland Bouvier (tc); John Cancalosi (br). **4–5 Alamy Stock Photo:** Dominique Braud / Dembinsky Photo Associates / Alamy; Bill Gozansky (Background). **5 Alamy Stock Photo:** Corbin17 (cra). **Science Photo Library:** Millard H. Sharp / Science Source (crb). **6–7 Alamy Stock Photo:** Bill Gozansky (Background). **6 Alamy Stock Photo:** ITAR-TASS News Agency (crb). **Dorling Kindersley:** Dorset Dinosaur Museum (cra). **Dreamstime.com:** Björn Wylezich (clb). **7 Alamy Stock Photo:** Chris Craggs (b). **Dorling Kindersley:** Natural History Museum, London (c). **Dreamstime.com:** Ken Backer (t). **8–9 Alamy Stock Photo:** Bill Gozansky (Background). **8 Science Photo Library:** Masato Hattori (cra). **9 Dorling Kindersley:** Natural History Museum, London (bl). **Dreamstime.com:** Fokinol (br). **10 Alamy Stock Photo:** The Natural History Museum, London (crb); Mervyn Rees (cr). **Dorling Kindersley:** Natural History Museum, London (cl); Naturmuseum Senckenburg, Frankfurt (bl). **Getty Images / iStock:** breckeni (c). **10–11 Alamy Stock Photo:** Bill Gozansky (Background). **11 Alamy Stock Photo:** Custom Life Science Images (tc); The Natural History Museum, London (c); Andrew Rubtsov (clb). **Dorling Kindersley:** Natural History Museum, London (tr). **Dreamstime.com:** Wellsie82 (br). **Getty Images / iStock:** Gerald Corsi (cr). **12–13 Alamy Stock Photo:** Bill Gozansky (Background). **Science Photo Library:** Alan Sirulnikoff. **13 123RF.com:** Galyna Andrushko (crb). **Alamy Stock Photo:** filmfoto-03edit (cr); Alan Sirulnikoff / All Canada Photos (cb). **Getty Images / iStock:** Elena Odareeva (cra). **14 123RF.com:** grafner (bc). **Dorling Kindersley:** Natural History Museum, London (cl). **Dreamstime.com:** Anton Starikov (cr). **14–15 Alamy Stock Photo:** Bill Gozansky (Background). **15 123RF.com:** Andreyoleynik (cr); koosen (ca). **Alamy Stock Photo:** Scott Camazine (cra). **Dreamstime.com:** Elena Schweitzer / Egal (br). **16–17 Alamy Stock Photo:** Bill Gozansky (Background). **16 Getty Images / iStock:** Ahorica (bl); oday222 (cr); Terryfic3D (br). **17 Dorling Kindersley:** Dorset Dinosaur Museum (tc); Natural History Museum, London (cla, ca); Natural History Museum (cra). **Dreamstime.com:** Amrkl5 (tr). **18 Alamy Stock Photo:** Jane Gould (bl); The Natural History Museum (c). **19 Alamy Stock Photo:** De Agostini Picture Library / Universal Images Group North America LLC (bl); tbkmedia.de (br). **Dorling Kindersley:** Natural History Museum, London (c). **20 123RF.com:** Mariusz Jurgielewicz (cl). **Alamy Stock Photo:** The Natural History Museum, London (c). **Dreamstime.com:** Corey A Ford (br). **21 Alamy Stock Photo:** blickwinkel / McPHOTO / PUW (c). **Dorling Kindersley:** Natural History Museum, London (br). **22 Alamy Stock Photo:** Susan E. Degginger (br); The Natural History Museum (bl). **Dreamstime.com:** Corey A Ford (cla). **23 Alamy Stock Photo:** The Natural History Museum (cl). Science Photo Library: Richard Bizley (br). **24 Alamy Stock Photo:** Chris Howes / Wild Places Photography (cla). **Dorling Kindersley:** Trustees of the National Museums Of Scotland (c). **Science Photo Library:** Mark P. Witton (br). **25 Alamy Stock Photo:** WaterFrame (br). **26 Alamy Stock Photo:** The Natural History Museum (c). **27 Dreamstime.com:** Lgor Dolgov / Id1974 (bc). **Science Photo Library:** Pascal Goetgheluck (cl); Natural History Museum, London (crb). **28 Getty Images / iStock:** Aunt_Spray (br). **29 Alamy Stock Photo:** blickwinkel / R. Koenig (br). **Science Photo Library:** Dirk Wiersma (c). **30 Alamy Stock Photo:** The Natural History Museum (bl). **Dreamstime.com:** Planetfelicity (c). **31 Dreamstime.com:** Corey A Ford (br); Planetfelicity (bl). **Science Photo Library:** US Department Of Energy (c). **32 Alamy Stock Photo:** The Natural History Museum, London (br); Tom Stack (cl). **32–33 Alamy Stock Photo:** Bill Gozansky (Background). **33 Alamy Stock Photo:** Martin Shields (cl). **Getty Images / iStock:** Bobainsworth (tr). **Science Photo Library:** Paul D Stewart (br). **34 Science Photo Library:** Biophoto Associates (c). **35 Alamy Stock Photo:** Paul R. Sterry / Nature Photographers Ltd (br); The Natural History Museum, London (c). **36 Alamy Stock Photo:** The Natural History Museum, London (cl). **Dorling Kindersley:** Natural History Museum, London (br). **37 Alamy Stock Photo:** Album (c). **Dreamstime.com:** Mark Turner (bc). **38 Alamy Stock Photo:** Mark A Schneider / Dembinsky Photo Associates (c); The Natural History Museum, London (br). **39 Alamy Stock Photo:** Heather Angel / Natural Visions (c). **Getty Images / iStock:** hsvrs (bl). **Science Photo Library:** Richard Bizley (br). **40 Alamy Stock Photo:** The Natural History Museum, London (cl). **40–41 Alamy Stock Photo:** Bill Gozansky (Background). **41 Alamy Stock Photo:** Phil Degginger (tr); The Natural History Museum, London (br). **Science Photo Library:** Pascal Goetgheluck (cl). **42 Alamy Stock Photo:** John Cancalosi (bl). **42–43 Alamy Stock Photo:** Roland Bouvier (bc); Corbin17 (tc); Bill Gozansky (Background). **43 Alamy Stock Photo:** B.A.E. Inc. (cra); Aleksandrs Kendenkovs (crb). **44–45 Alamy Stock Photo:** Bill Gozansky (Background). **44 Alamy Stock Photo:** GL Archive (cra); The Natural History Museum, London (clb). **Dorling Kindersley:** Natural History Museum, London (bc, cr). **45 Alamy Stock Photo:** CNP Collection (br); Pictorial Press Ltd (cla); GL Archive (tr, clb). **Dorling Kindersley:** Dorset Dinosaur Museum (tc); Natural History Museum, London (bl); Staatliches Museum fur Naturkunde (cr). **46 Alamy Stock Photo:** The Natural History Museum, London (cl, c). **Science Photo Library:** Dirk Wiersma (bc). **47 Alamy Stock Photo:** Ryan M. Bolton (bl). **Dorling Kindersley:** Natural History Museum, London (c). **48 Alamy Stock Photo:** WaterFrame (c). **Dreamstime.com:** Mr1805 (br). **49 Alamy Stock Photo:** Walter Myers / Stocktrek Images (br). **Science Photo Library:** Millard H. Sharp (c). **50 Alamy Stock Photo:** Corbin17 (c). **Getty Images / iStock:** Christophe Sirabella (bc). **51 Alamy Stock Photo:** The Natural History Museum, London (c). **Dreamstime.com:** Siloto (bc). **Science Photo Library:** Millard H. Sharp / Science Source (br). **52 Alamy Stock Photo:** Kevin Schafer / Avalon.red (l). **Getty Images / iStock:** wwing (br). **53 Alamy Stock Photo:** Corbin17 (c). **Dorling Kindersley:** Natural History Museum, London (cra). **54 Dreamstime.com:** Daniel Eskridge (bc); Russell Shively / Trilobite (br). **Getty Images:** Wild Horizons / Universal Images (c). **55 Alamy Stock Photo:** Mohamad Haghani (cr). **Science Photo Library:** Millard H. Sharp (cb). **Shutterstock.com:** topimages (bc). **56 Alamy Stock Photo:** Natural Visions / Heather Angel (c); Panther Media GmbH / MIROXXXX (br). **57 Dreamstime.com:** Planetfelicity (bc); Yezhenliang (c). **58 Dorling Kindersley:** Oxford Museum of Natural History (b). **58–59 Alamy Stock Photo:** Agefotostock / Tolo Balaguer (bc); Bill Gozansky (Background). **Dorling Kindersley:** Oxford Museum of Natural History (t). **59 123RF.com:** Mark Turner (cb). **Getty Images:** Toronto Star / Bernard Weil (b). **60 Dorling Kindersley:** Natural History Museum, London (clb); Trustees of the Natural History Museum, London (c). **61 Dorling Kindersley:** Senckenberg Gesellschaft Fuer Naturforschung Museum (c). **Dreamstime.com:** Mark Turner (br). **62 Dorling Kindersley:** Courtesy of Dorset Dinosaur Museum (clb). **62–63 Alamy Stock Photo:** Bill Gozansky (Background); The Natural History Museum, London (b). **63 Alamy Stock Photo:** NDK (crb). Dorling Kindersley: Natural History Museum (tl); Natural History Museum, London (cra). **64 Alamy Stock Photo:** Gabbro; Mohamad Haghani (bl). **65 Alamy Stock Photo:** MShieldsPhotos (c). **Dreamstime.com:** Corey A Ford (bc). **66 Dorling Kindersley:** Royal Tyrrell Museum of Palaeontology, Alberta, Canada (c). **67 Alamy Stock Photo:** Stocktrek Images, Inc. / Jose Antonio Penas (br). **Dorling Kindersley:** Royal Tyrrell Museum of Palaeontology, Alberta, Canada (c). **68 Alamy Stock Photo:** Puwadol Jaturawutthichai (c); Stocktrek Images, Inc. / Mohamad Haghani (bc). **Dreamstime.com:** Panupong Ponchai (br). **69 Alamy Stock Photo:** Mohamad Haghani (br). **Getty Images / iStock:** Crazytang (c). **Science Photo Library:** Dirk Wiersma (cla). **70 Alamy Stock Photo:** Natural Visions / Heather Angel (br). **Dorling Kindersley:** Senckenberg Nature Museum (c). **Dreamstime.com:** Isselee (bl). **71 Alamy Stock Photo:** Minden Pictures / Kevin Schafer (c). **72 Alamy Stock Photo:** The Natural History Museum, London. **Science Photo Library:** Jaime Chirinos (br). **73 Trustees of the Natural History Museum, London:** (c). **Science Photo Library:** Roman Uchytel (bc). **74–75 Alamy Stock Photo:** Bill Gozansky (Background); Mohamad Haghani. **75 Alamy Stock Photo:** Phil Degginger (br); Zachary Frank (cra). **Science Photo Library:** Millard H. Sharp (crb). **76 Dorling Kindersley:** Natural History Museum, London (cb). **77 Dorling Kindersley:** Natural History Museum, London (br). **Science Photo Library:** Mauricio Anton (bc); Millard H. Sharp (c). **78 123RF.com:** Andrea (bl). **Alamy Stock Photo:** Phil Degginger (c); Universal Images Group North America LLC / DeAgostini Picture Library (br). **79 Alamy Stock Photo:** Arterra Picture Library / Clement Philippe (bl); James Jagger. **Dorling Kindersley:** Jon Hughes (cra). **80 Alamy Stock Photo:** Q-Images (c). **Dreamstime.com:** Suljo (br). **Science Photo Library:** Michael Long (bc). **81 Alamy Stock Photo:** Ryan M. Bolton (bl); Maurice Savage (c). **82 Alamy Stock Photo:** The Natural History Museum, London (c, br). **Science Photo Library:** James Kuether (bc). **83 Dorling Kindersley:** Oxford Museum of Natural History (r). **Science Photo Library:** John Reader (bl). **84 Alamy Stock Photo:** The Natural History Museum, London (ca); Rick Rudnicki (bl, br). **84–85 Alamy Stock Photo:** Bill Gozansky (Background). **85 Dorling Kindersley:** Oxford Museum of Natural History (cb). **Dreamstime.com:** Mark Turner (br). **Getty Images / iStock:** E+ / benedek (tl). **Science Photo Library:** Steve Gschmeissner (tr). **86 Alamy Stock Photo:** Xinhua (cb). Di-Ying Huang: (ca). Trustees of the Natural History Museum, London: (br). **86–87 Alamy Stock Photo:** Bill Gozansky (Background). **87 Alamy Stock Photo:** blickwinkel / Jagel (br); Rick Rudnicki (c). **Shutterstock.com:** Tarakanbix (tc). **88 123RF.com:** Petra Schüller / pixelelfe (cr). **Getty Images / iStock:** Marccophoto (cla). **88–89 Alamy Stock Photo:** Bill Gozansky (Background). **Dorling Kindersley:** Natural History Museum, London (b). **Dreamstime.com:** Feathercollector (tc). **89 Getty Images / iStock:** Mark Kostich (cla). **90 Alamy Stock Photo:** Album (fcrb); The Natural History Museum, London (cla/ Zamites, fcr, cb/Archimedes, crb, bc/Dactylioceras, fbr); blickwinkel / McPHOTO / PUW (ca/Pecopteris); The Natural History Museum (fcla, ca, ca/Porana, fcl, c/Hallucigenia); Tom Stack (cr); Martin Shields (clb); Heather Angel / Natural Visions (bl); Mark A Schneider / Dembinsky Photo Associates (fbl); Phil Degginger (bc). **Dorling Kindersley:** Trustees of the National Museums Of Scotland (cra); Natural History Museum, London (cla). **Getty Images / iStock:** Bobainsworth (fclb). **Science Photo Library:** Biophoto Associates (cb/ Pterygotus); Pascal Goetgheluck (cl, br); Dirk Wiersma (c); US Department Of Energy (ca/Tullimonstrum); Paul D Stewart (cb). **90–91 Alamy Stock Photo:** Bill Gozansky (Background). **91 Alamy Stock Photo:** Kevin Schafer / Avalon.red (tr); The Natural History Museum, London (tc/Eryops, ftl, cra, fcrb, br); Corbin17 (ftr, tc/Tiktaalik); WaterFrame (tl/Coccosteus); Natural Visions / Heather Angel (cla/ Scaphognathus); Puwadol Jaturawutthichai (fclb); NDK (c); Gabbro (c/ Patagotitan); MShieldsPhotos (c/Khaan); Phil Degginger (bl); Q-Images (bc); James Jagger (bc/Coelodonta); Maurice Savage (bc/Mammuthus). **Dorling Kindersley:** Courtesy of Dorset Dinosaur Museum (fcra); Natural History Museum, London (tl, cl, cb/Morganucodon); Senckenberg Gesellschaft Fuer Naturforschung Museum (ca); Trustees of the Natural History Museum, London (ca/Stegosaurus); Natural History Museum (fcl); Royal Tyrrell Museum of Palaeontology, Alberta, Canada (cr, fcr); Senckenberg Nature Museum (cb); Oxford Museum of Natural History (fbr). **Dreamstime.com:** Yezhenliang (ca/platecarpus). **Getty Images / iStock:** Crazytang (clb). **Getty Images:** Wild Horizons / Universal Images (fcla). Trustees of the Natural History Museum, London: (crb). **Science Photo Library:** Millard H. Sharp (tc, cla, fbl). **92 Getty Images / iStock:** Gerald Corsi (br). **Science Photo Library:** Masato Hattori (tr). **92–93 Alamy Stock Photo:** Bill Gozansky (Background). **93 Alamy Stock Photo:** The Natural History Museum, London (br). **94 Dreamstime.com:** Planetfelicity (b). **Trustees of the Natural History Museum, London:** (t). **94–95 Alamy Stock Photo:** Bill Gozansky (Background). **95 Alamy Stock Photo:** MShieldsPhotos (br). **96 Alamy Stock Photo:** Bill Gozansky (Background). **Dr Dean Lomax:** Brian Fernando (br).

**Cover images:** *Front:* **Alamy Stock Photo:** blickwinkel / McPHOTO / PUW br, Roland Bouvier ca, John Cancalosi fcra, Corbin17 crb, James Jagger tc, The Natural History Museum bc, The Natural History Museum, London ftl, ca/ (toenails), cra, cr, cb, Martin Shields tl; **Dorling Kindersley:** Courtesy of Dorset Dinosaur Museum cb/ (skin), Dorset Dinosaur Museum fcrb, Natural History Museum, London cl, clb; **Dreamstime.com:** Panupong Ponchai fcrb/ (skeleton), Björn Wylezich bl; **Science Photo Library:** Biophoto Associates crb/ (Eurypterid), Natural History Museum, London cla; *Back:* **Alamy Stock Photo:** Album ca/ (dragonfly), Mark A Schneider / Dembinsky Photo Associates fcla, Kevin Schafer / Avalon.red crb, John Cancalosi cra, MShieldsPhotos ftl, The Natural History Museum cb/ (Porana), The Natural History Museum, London cr, clb, fbl, NDK ca, Q-Images tr, Universal Images Group North America LLC / DeAgostini Picture Library tc; **Dorling Kindersley:** br, Natural History Museum, London tl, Oxford Museum of Natural History bl, Royal Tyrrell Museum of Palaeontology, Alberta, Canada cl; **Dreamstime.com:** Feathercollector fcla/ (Feather), Fokinol cla; **Science Photo Library:** Pascal Goetgheluck fclb, Dirk Wiersma cb; *Spine:* **Alamy Stock Photo:** The Natural History Museum, London ca/ (toenails), cb; **Dorling Kindersley:** Courtesy of Dorset Dinosaur Museum b, Natural History Museum, London ca.



## About the author

Dr. Dean Lomax is a paleontologist, TV presenter, and author. He has loved dinosaurs since he was a child and is now a world expert on ichthyosaurs—having named five new species. He often appears as an expert on TV and has also written *My Book of Dinosaurs and Prehistoric Life* for DK.